THE ULTIMATE EXPERIENCE
THE MANY PATHS TO GOD

YOUR SPACE BROTHERS
and
SISTERS GREET YOU!

Presenters: Our Father-Christ Michael, Lords Yeshua, Ashtar, Djwhal Khul, Korton, Andromeda Rex, Surea of Sirius, and Divine Mother, Lady Nada, Tuella, Quan Yin.

BOOK SIX
VERLING CHAKO PRIEST, PhD

Proof-books 1
no Preface!
3-12-08
Chako's Copy

Cover layout by Author.

Order this book online at www.trafford.com/07-2886
or email orders@trafford.com

Most Trafford titles are also available at major online book retailers.

Note for Librarians: A cataloguing record for this book is available from Library
and Archives Canada at www.collectionscanada.ca/amicus/index-e.html

Printed in Victoria, BC, Canada.

ISBN: 978-1-4251-6302-0

*We at Trafford believe that it is the responsibility of us all, as both individuals
and corporations, to make choices that are environmentally and socially sound.
You, in turn, are supporting this responsible conduct each time you purchase a
Trafford book, or make use of our publishing services. To find out how you are
helping, please visit www.trafford.com/responsiblepublishing.html*

*Our mission is to efficiently provide the world's finest, most comprehensive
book publishing service, enabling every author to experience success.
To find out how to publish your book, your way, and have it available
worldwide, visit us online at www.trafford.com/10510*

 **Trafford** PUBLISHING™ **www.trafford.com**

North America & international
toll-free: 1 888 232 4444 (USA & Canada)
phone: 250 383 6864 ♦ fax: 250 383 6804 ♦ email: info@trafford.com

The United Kingdom & Europe
phone: +44 (0)1865 722 113 ♦ local rate: 0845 230 9601
facsimile: +44 (0)1865 722 868 ♦ email: info.uk@trafford.com

10 9 8 7 6 5 4 3 2 1

DEDICATION

I dedicate this Book Six to my
Space Brothers and Sisters.
And E-li'sha prayed and said, Lord, I pray
thee, open his eyes that he may see. And the
Lord opened the eyes of the young man and he
behold, the mountain was full of...
chariots of fire... *(2 Kings 6:17)*

ACKNOWLEDGMENTS

I once again give many thanks and appreciation to the Father, Lord Yeshua, and the many Presenters who came forth and made this book possible. Their enthusiasm for this coming project of the spaceships' landing and then offering to lift-off those of us who choose this way of leaving the planet for the duration of the coming Earth changes is palpable. They will shower us with their love and who of us can resist that?

I give thanks to my dear friend and editor, Heather Clarke. She is a stalwart soul with seemingly tireless energy and frequently was editing my work into the wee hours of morning. She is the founder of the *Arizona Enlightenment Center* in Goodyear, Arizona. It is our dream to establish a large complex where people may come for rejuvenation and to hear about or learn esoteric modalities—a spiritual spa of sorts. We will do this with God's help!

Susan Verling Miller O'Brien is not only my first born, but my *hands-on* help when framing my books. Whenever I got into a computer glitch, for I was learning a new system with my HP lap-top, she was able to find the problem that I had created and get me back on track. She is still the person creating the headers and footers, although I am now able to do some of that. Thank you, dear heart!

Last, but not least, I give thanks to you Readers who buy, read, and email me how you love the books.

Blessings!

PREFACE

Where to begin? This has been an incredible journey for me. It all started back in August 2002 when I felt this soft finger caress my cheek. The room became electrified as the Entity spoke lovingly to me. It was Lord Sananda making contact after I had questioned who was speaking telepathically to me. When I asked him if he were Jesus, he replied, *No, but he is an aspect of me!* I was stunned and had to take a warm shower to help stabilize my body. Now, five years and six books later I understand the meaning of his coming to me. I was to write books!

It has been a profound learning experience for me. The Masters gave me the main title of the books and then differentiated them by using sub-titles. I am a Virgo and tend to obsess over the exactness of literary grammar— *never end a sentence with a proposition, etcetera.* That is quite evident with the first three books. There was not a natural flow with the words, and they seemed stilted to me —artificially dignified. (Those first three books are not available, nor have an ISBN#.) Consequently, I have loosened up a bit and follow the suggestions of my editor.

I never quite know what to expect when starting a book. The Masters do not give me the sub-title even until the book's theme is well established. It allows for flexibility to be woven into the theme. They do not even give me a hint as to the nature of a new book that is on the horizon, for they have remarked that I would start writing it for them (*smile*). Ah yes, they know me well.

Your Space Brothers and Sisters Greet You!
PREFACE

You can imagine my surprise when Yeshua brought in Commander Ashtar, and they almost immediately made reference to spaceships. They not only reference them, but lead the Readers step by step to being offered safe passage on them—*lift-offs are your freedom of choice.*

Eleven Presenters come forth and give their wisdom on current affairs of America and go on to describe what one can expect on board a spaceship of Light. Keep an open mind, Readers, for much of the information is literally out of this world (*smile*).

As you read the chapters, you will note that there will be italic print. This is to alert you that Yeshua and I are making some comments before and after the channeling. My remarks will be differentiated further by parentheses. I also use italic print to let you know a particular emotion I feel as they are giving me a transmission (*chuckles*).

I have been questioned before as to whether what *you* read is what I have heard verbatim. I give you a qualified YES, for while my editor, Heather, and I do modify the material slightly—changing *So to Therefore, or But to However*—we maintain the integrity of the transmissions that we pass on to you to the best of our ability.

Fasten your seat belts, Readers. You are about to take an extraordinary journey as you explore the pages of this book. Rest assured that we too have experienced every emotion that you will feel. Open your hearts and meet all of us between the pages. Blessings, Chako

TABLE OF CONTENTS

INTRODUCTION

Good morning, dearest one, **I Am Yeshua,** *back once again. Yes, I am truly he. We have much to discuss this morning, for I wish to start the Introduction of this book that you are calling Book SIX. We have decided that the title is to remain the same. As we previously have said, Book FIVE was to be the last book in that series. And it* **is** *of that nature. However, this new book will still retain the title,* The Ultimate Experience: The Many Paths to God. *We are merely naming more ways that people can come to God.*

For those who are not familiar with this way of thinking, if you have me, Yeshua, you will know that there will be teachings to help you find your way to God. Our Father is the most loving of all Energies on Earth.

Many people may wonder at the vastness of this Universe. They may wonder at the vastness of this world that they live in. It is a sphere of Light and dark. It is a duality that was set up to let humanity play out its karmic games. That is coming to a close, for as this precious Earth moves into the fifth dimension, she no longer will tolerate Beings on her that are of the dark. They are being removed, and if you do not have that separation between Light and dark, the duality also will then start to lessen.

In the beginning of your linear time as you know it, many souls were born onto this planet for the opportunity to play out their karma, as I have said. Now not all karma is of the negative; this you must know, for you can have beautiful relationships where you have come together in great love that stemmed from the fact that you have had beautiful pasts together. Therefore, that would be your

1

positive karma. Those who are in the helping professions have had positive karma from the past and love the work that they do.

Therefore, the previous way of interacting on Earth with your karmic problems and your Akashic records are drawing to a close. This must happen, for you are coming into the fifth dimension. In that dimension things are looked at differently. There is more appreciation for people, relationships, and even for the things that you already have. There is less materiality thinking. People wonder why there is so much distrust of others. Those who are causing this are in that third dimension, and they are in the process of ending those third-dimensional games. They will be coming into the fourth dimension, which is a transition period before entering into the fifth. In our fourth book, we talked a great deal about dimensions. For you new Readers, go to the fourth book and read about dimensions. (Realities of the Crucifixion.)

Now why am I bringing all of this up again? To gradually make the transition into this book. We have set this book up in a somewhat similar fashion, but at the same time it will be different, of course, for it is a new book. We will be bringing in different people to speak. Again they have graciously accepted our invitation to step forth. These new Presenters will be just that—new ones. This book will not have a religious overtone to it. That part is finished. As we have said that was the end of that series.

In this book, we shall be bringing you into modern times, closer times toward 2012. Think back when there was so much hoopla surrounding the coming millennium of 2000. It was a propitious time in history. However, seven years have passed, and when you think back on it, there is not much difference from your 1990's. You still have your weather conditions. You still have your earthquakes and

2

your tsunamis here and there. You still have your wars and killings, rapes, degenerate thinking. Nothing much has changed, has it? It seems to go on.

Now you are at 2007—almost at the end of it, moving ever closer to 2012. It is the time of ending of cycle, actually, for those of the dark are given the choice to come to the Light or they will be sent to another planet or another sphere-space which Christians would call their Hell. It is of their own choosing.

There will be many great changes to the topography of the Earth. This must happen. She is changing her clothes. She is putting on a new suit of clothes. Just like what you do—you bathe yourself, you wash yourself and you clean off all the energies that have collected upon you. It is the same with her. She shakes and rattles. The storms wash her; the oceans wash her. She shakes off the dark ones and they make their transitions.

Many people will be leaving, for they have had it. It is an interesting fact that while in Nirvana you can stay and play and not have to come back right away. However, you will come again, for it is the progression, the evolution of the soul that must continue.

I wish to address now how we have set this book up. This is the Introduction chapter and there will be Beings that come to speak in this chapter. Whether you believe what they say or not is for you to discern. Whether you believe their truth or not is for you to discern. It is the way of all books. You read it and there are kernels of wisdom throughout. You chew on those kernels and you digest them. Before you know it, they have become part of your wisdom.

I Am Jesus the Christ. Christ is a title. The Creator of this Universe is known as Christ Michael. Sananda is a

*Christ. A Christ is one of the Light that has earned the title through wisdom and purity of thought, love—love of humanity and love of self, for you must **be** love, acknowledge that you are love in order to be a Christ.*

Most of you know that when I walked your Earth I was learning about humanity, what it was to be human. I experienced everything. I experienced love and hate, punishment and torture. I experienced marriage and fatherhood. Whether you believe that or not is up to you. I experienced old age. I experienced different religions. I experienced mystical schools of thought and Initiations. I experienced all of this so that I could bring it back to the Father. He was in me and I was in Him. I was the Son and He was the Father. I can carry this a step further. I became Him.

How many of you in your human lives and as you grow into your old age have heard, "she is just like her mother; or he is just like his father?" You see it is carried on. You become your mother or you become your father. You see that it happened to me at a younger age than most of you. It happened to me at the time of my baptism by John the Baptist. I became Divine at that point. I was my Father. Many Christians believe this; many Jews abhor this. The belief systems of the many...

During the time that this Channel is open to me and my teachings, we fill her with the Presence of God. She becomes a spokesperson for us. This book will have a different tone and what I have just said will not be repeated. It was merely for the Introduction. The Biblical players in the other books, the Marys and the Apostles will not have center stage in this book. We are changing focus and wishing to help humanity for what is to come. The format will stay the same where the Author and I will have

4

our little conversations before and after the chapters. There will be approximately twenty chapters.

Now without further words from me, I will step aside and let some of the Presenters step forward and present themselves in this introductory chapter. The next person will be a familiar one for you. He has been around his Galactic world for many an eon. I will step aside now and let him begin. (9-29-07)

Good morning to you Readers and to this Channel. **I AM Ashtar** of the Galactic Command. We have told this Channel in the past that I would come and download much information to her. This we are in the process of doing. You know that when you are filling a sparkling vessel with fluid waters of information, you pour it in slowly, for you do not wish to bring in a gush of information that could be *destructive* to the body. Therefore, we bring it in in a gentle way.

This book is in preparation for what is to come. As we talk in the next chapters, we will discuss it at more depth. We are coming, dear friends. We of the Galactic Federation of Light are coming. We will be landing on your shores, but we come with such Light and peace and love that it is hoped that you will receive us as such and not go into fear.

We think it is probably a psychological response when you have not seen anything like we will be doing and the body goes into fear. That could stem from past life experiences way back, thousands of years back, 25,000 years back where the cells in the bodies still remember what you thought were strange happenings.

Our ships have many descriptions and designs. It all depends on what planet they are from—the Pleiadians,

Sirians, Arcturians all have their own designs. If you wish to read more on this, by all means go to the website of that great Sirian Commander himself, Sheldan Nidle (www.paoweb.com). He also has a video called *Landings 101* that will give you a great description of what that first landing will be like.

You see we are not coming to capture you, but to give you our technology, to give you our love, our peace. Think back when you had something exciting to share. You could hardly wait to share it. That is the way it has been with us. We see you struggle with your technology, and we are so excited and we say *we have this; we can show you*! We have advanced technology that we could show you. How would you like to just push a button and have your meal appear! We have so much information that we could give you.

One of the most difficult tasks for humanity may be to learn our protocol. You see there is a protocol that you *must* recognize and you *must* agree to, for it is for your own protection. Just as you have been taught to never touch a live electrical wire dangling down from a power source, you must learn when it is safe to approach one of our ships. It is because we use radiation for technical purposes. If you approached too soon, you could be burned.

Your movies have shown a good example when a craft crashes that there is this big hole or there are burnt trees, or scorched earth. That is from the heat of the metal and the radiation. We must turn all of that off after we come gently down. It is similar to your airplanes. You come gently down and then the pilot turns off the engines. Then the people can debark or embark.

It is the same with us. Do not come close until we signal that it is safe for you. And NO we are not of the *grays* that will capture you and experiment on you. That is so primitive and not our purpose. Therefore, dear Readers, you see you will have these instructions that you must follow.

Another teaching that we will give out will be to your governments and your military. Again your movies depict a space ship surrounded by all the guns and tanks all pointed at it. We come in peace. Why would you shoot us? It is always from fear, you see. When one is in fear, that is when the dark can come in and say *shoot that person; he is going to kill you!* That is not so; that is not so.

We will be bringing love, camaraderie, and joy, love, and peace. Please accept us. Please give your love back to us and project no fear. We will not harm you in any way. We will provide tours. These are not the great Mother ships that land, for they are miles and miles across. You would not have the accommodations for such huge ships. Picture a ship that is many times bigger than your football fields. Where would it land? It could not. A smaller Mother ship could land at an airport, but there could not be any other planes around it, for the space ship is so huge it would touch all the buildings and other planes in the vicinity.

You see our ships can be many miles across. They can be like a village or city inside of them, so we come in the smaller ships and not in the huge Mother ships. However, we offer tours in our smaller ships where you can see the banks of computers that make it all happen. We will give you banquets of food—foods that you have never tasted before that are delicious and nutritious and good for you.

We can show you areas that we have for meditation, where we can find the Father's Presence even more strongly. We can sit there and commune with Him and talk with Him. You might call it a Chapel, but to us they are meditation rooms. We have several aboard, of course, because the ships are large.

We will show you our Conference rooms and how we set those up. They could be similar to your classrooms at a University. There are computer screens that drop down by the seats. All of this might be interesting for you.

We can show you our libraries where we have books to study. Your tours will be free—you will not have to pay in order to get in (*smile*).

It will be a glorious time, and we look forward to it. It will happen, dear Readers. It will happen before 2012.

I will now step aside because another waits. I will speak with you throughout the pages of this book. Thank you for this privilege. There is more to come. I AM Ashtar.

Good morning to you Readers and to this Channel. It is my great privilege to be invited to be a participant in this book. Perhaps you know me as **Korton.** I am from Mars. I am the Communicator; I am the radio station for the Fleet. I keep a direct communication between the many ships in the Ashtar Command. When the ships land, it will be because I have ascertained that it is safe to do so. I follow the thoughts of humanity. I am able to see what is in their hearts.

Not everyone, of course, will greet us with open arms. That is human nature, and we take that into consideration. It has been questioned about our stations on Mars. It is thought by your scientists who see only the obvious—a dry, hot planet, a red planet without water—that there can be no living people on it. But you see they are only looking through third dimension eyes.

Mars is very populated in its inner core—very similar to Earth's (*inner earth*). We have purposely put our radio stations underground in order to keep them safe—not only from Earthlings, but also from those marauders from other planets who come to check us out.

This Channel has been drawn to watch some of those science-fiction television shows. She is particularly fond of watching *Stargate, SG-1*. It has very similar episodes as to what goes on with us. It is called a *Stargate* in the television series and that is similar to what we do, for we move from one dimension to another through what is known as a *Stargate*.

People will be suspicious and will not take kindly to our coming. And even though I am on Mars, I will definitely be on one of those first ships. Humanity does not realize just how much history we will be creating when we land. It has been thousands of years since we have done so. That would be during your Lemurian and Atlantian times when there were ships that came and went. The Mayans all knew of us. The Egyptians in their pyramids all knew of us. Those pyramids were created way before scientists said they were. They were created by thoughts that moved the great stones for communication purposes—chambers within chambers. Even to this day not all have been discovered, for we are speaking of dimensions again.

When the Earth has entered fully into the fifth dimension, there will be more chambers discovered in the pyramids. They will suddenly be able to find them with their instruments. People do not realize that many things reside in different dimensions that one cannot see now,

because of Earth's present dimension—3D, we like to say—
that is going into the fourth dimension, 4D.

There are people of course in the fifth dimension,
but it is difficult to remain so when one is constantly
bombarded by the lower vibrations of much of humanity.
This Channel must reside in the fifth and into the sixth in
order for us to clearly communicate with her. It is a
struggle even for her, as she gets caught up in the
physicality of just living on Earth.

When we come, the angels will sound their
trumpets. Whether all of humanity hears this or not will be
according to where their consciousness resides. Those of a
higher awareness will hear it. Those of less awareness will
not, for they will be in their fear, you see. It amazes us how
one can be afraid of something just because it is different.

We of the Galactic Command move throughout the
planets and Universes. And yes, there is more than one
Universe in case people do not know this. You go into
different Universes and different planets and there are
different life forms. As Sheldan Nidle has said in his video
Landings 101, some of the Beings are quite lovely to look
at while others are not quite as appealing to our eyesight.
However, after you have been in the work that we have
been for eons of time, there is not much that surprises us.
Even different body shapes can carry brilliant minds and we
have come to respect this and to honor them, for some are
ancient beyond one's reality.

Communication is so important. We communicate
with thought and it is transferred to our computers. We use
lights and crystals and magnificent stones—what you
would call *jewels.* We use these in the proper way, the way
of Light consciousness. We do not possess any of them.
We do not covet any of them. We do not hoard any of

them. There is no greed on board the ships of Light. There is only beauty and love.

Many people do not understand what true love is, for love can be caring and adoring. However, it can be a strong emotion, fierce in its protectiveness, as is displayed with a mother and her child. Love can be that emotion where it can look like that tough love where a parent must address a child's predilection to drugs. It takes a strong, fiercely loving parent to turn those children into conscious Beings.

All of this is part of our communication. We practice that fierce way of loving. People do not realize that there are still such events that you call *Star Wars*. There are fierce battles on the ground and in the air. If a particular planet has water, fierce battles could take place in its oceans, using weapons that you have not even heard of before — that you have no vocabulary for. It is beyond what most people's finite minds could even think of. Yes, Readers, those wars still go on.

However, you see our Fleet of millions of ships surround the grid of Earth. There are many marauders that would love to come to Earth and rape its land of resources, take its crystals, take its waters, take its oils, take its gold and metals, rape it and leave it a dry shell. This has happened to other planets in the past. It has killed that Being, for planets of course are living Beings; or they are dead.

Now you have been taught that all of you are Creations of God and are finding your way back Home. This you can do, but you must raise your vibratory rates. You must eat properly; you must rest properly; you must play and bring joy into your life.

Many people have different ideas as to what joy is. For many, it is going to Disneyland. To others it is going to beautiful islands and basking on the sands and playing in the oceans. For others, it is writing a book—this Channel feels much joy in this process of bringing forth a book. And it gives us much joy to be able to participate.

The Lord Yeshua is orchestrating this book, as he has done with the previous ones. This book is an introduction to worlds out there. There are millions of ships out there, Readers. Each has a different story. Each is communicating through banks and banks of computers. Many are relayed through me, Korton from Mars.

I will now close this segment and wish all of you Readers God speed, and I will look forward to meeting you when our ships land on your shores.

Thank you, I am Korton (*Thank you, Korton, it was a privilege for me.*) And for me.

All right, dear one, shall we call it a day? (Yes, I think this would be a good time to finish up.) Then this is it for today, dear one. Over and out. (Thank you, Lord.)

Good morning, I am Yeshua and a new Presenter is coming forth. I will let him introduce himself.

Good morning to our Readers. I am the next Presenter in line. **I AM Andromeda Rex.** I have not come before, therefore this Channel does not know me per se, but she does know my name. I am in the Ashtar Command, and I have much to do with the energies that flow around Earth and therefore around the Command. I help regulate these energies. I help the grids of Earth stay stable. I help the fire in the volcanoes to calm down. I help fault lines to become more stable. I am not the only one, of course, for there are many. However, we all have a hand in keeping Earth on an even keel. As you have been told, she is raising her vibration and therefore these Earth changes that you all most likely have heard about must come to fruition.

I know it must seem as if we are crying wolf. When Tuella put out her little booklets and communiques back in the 1980's, one could say that that was 27 years ago when we were preparing humanity for a possible lift-off. That has been neutralized somewhat. The Elohim have managed to keep all of that from happening so far. However, it is to the point where the rubber band can be stretched just so far. The finger in the dike can plug the hole just so long. The energies build and build until there must be a release.

If you will notice, many times there will be movies and television shows that start to play the theme of volcanoes or earthquakes. You see, we impress upon them to get the old films out of the archives and play them again. It then can become a wakeup call for people.

People on the west coast have heard about the *Big One* and yet it has been almost a century it seems and nothing has happened. It will happen. Many of you have gone through strife in past lives. You are not immune to all of this. Many of you went through Lemuria and Atlantis. Your memories of those ancient times of 25,000 years or so ago are in your body. Your body remembers this.

Therefore, there are times when your body will be afraid when you hear about any of the coming events. You easily can go into fear, for it sparks the remembrance that is in the cells. This is where you need to practice emotional stability. You need to practice mental stability and keep your body grounded. As we watch humanity, there are many people still releasing their third dimensional consciousness. They do not believe in space ships. They

13

are loyal to the government and do not believe in governmental conspiracies, let alone that there could be murders of any kind. They only see that in movies and do not believe that perhaps some of that could be true.

It is time, Readers, to know that perhaps there could be an element of truth in everything you see and hear. It does not mean that it is all truth, but keep an open mind and know that there can be streams of truth through much of what you are reading and what you have been told. There is that saying "an ounce of truth and a pound of lies." The media will refute much of the truth, for it is coming down from the top, and they must do so in order to keep their jobs. When they refute something, that is the thread of truth that they are covering up. Understand that and you will be well on your way to a different consciousness.

This book is for the awakening of people. We wish to convey to you that there is much out there, as we will put it, that is truth. This book will not be Biblical, but one certainly could match what is said with the prophecies in the Bible, even though those Bibles have also been distorted. I and others watch the energies. We watch the energies that are emitted from the natural sources of Earth and from the people of Earth. We monitor.

There has been so much dramatization on a negative order how the aliens, the *grays* as they are called, come and can experiment on people and can destroy Earth. That is all fear propaganda. Because of this type of mentality, we have much that we need to address. Humanity has much to un-learn with an open mind. The dark opposition has done a clever job in thrusting fear upon humanity. However, let me give you a picture of truth—a picture that you can hold in your hearts with joy.

Picture a large ship shimmering in its effervescence and opulence, looking like a giant mother of pearl object slowly coming down from your Heavens. Hear the hum, a tone emitting from it. Notice the silence as it makes that first contact with Earth's soil and the engines are stilled. Picture a door appearing, a door that was not in evidence before and silently is being lifted up and disappearing into the ship. Picture a Being coming forth in all his glory. They do not call him the *Radiant One* for nothing! He will be wearing a space suit that looks metallic — shining material. The love and the frequency that flows from him is magnificent. Hear the trumpets sound as the angels announce his coming. You Christians who prayed for the coming of the Christ, here he is, shining in all his glory. At that moment, humanity will feel no fear, but only awe and reverence. Many will fall to their knees, as he stands before them on a platform that has glided out from the ship. He will address the crowd and with his arms raised will bless them. He will then re-enter the ship while his emissaries come forth and talk to the crowd.

This is what you have to look forward to, dear Readers — a day that will burn in your memory cells and last you lifetimes, lifetime after lifetime. Those of you who were with him in those ancient times and remember him on the Mount will know that here he is again, as promised. He is known as the **Radiant One** throughout the Universes. He is known as Lord Sananda Kumara, the Holy One, Esu. The experience will be one that will be written in your history books and people who come after you will read about this for generations onwards.

I now will close. I AM Andromeda Rex. (Thank you, Lord.)

All right, dear one, does this do it? (I think so, Lord.) Andromeda Rex is the Being that watches your shores. Until tomorrow, dear one, adieu.

Good morning, Readers and to this Channel. I Am Yeshua bringing forth another Presenter for the Introduction of our book. Without further comments from me, I will step aside and let her speak.

Readers and Channel, I am so delighted to be able to be here for the launching of this new book. You do not know me that well, actually, but I know all of you quite well. **I AM Lady Master Nada.** I am the twin flame of your Lord, the one they call the *Radiant One.* Together, we are quite a flaming pair!

I have been asked to speak, simply because I am so greatly involved with the ships. Of course, since Sananda has his ship, I am there also. What I want to speak with you Readers about is that during this book there will be new ideas given to you—new concepts that perhaps you have never thought about. The purpose of this book is to awaken those people who hold these memories of being on the ships.

Another purpose is that for any of you new Readers, those doubters or those ones who think that UFOs are alien and are not to be trusted, that perhaps by reading this you will begin to know us as the loving Beings that we are. In our ships, the atmosphere is one of love and caring and peace. While some of our ships are in other Universes and are more of the military bent, there is still reverence and love for God inside the ships. We travel all over the Universes in our service to the Heavenly One, known to many as Christ Michael, or God the Father, God the Mother—not to forget the Goddess energies.

Let us talk about Earth. Let us talk about what one may expect in the next few years. You know there is a countdown. Someone wrote on the Internet that perhaps 2012 will be looked upon as nothing more than a *bad hair day!* I beg to differ (*chuckles*); I beg to differ. It has a purpose, for it is the *ending* of a particular era. The Mayans called it the *end of the world,* but at the same time they knew it was a beginning.

The worlds go on continuously. And yes, there comes a time perhaps when a particular planet dies off. But for you on Earth, people, you can forget about that for a while. It is not going to happen for billions and billions of years. Just be more or less in the present here, for 2012 is approaching quite swiftly. Since 2007 is almost completed, we now are talking about 2008. There are only four more years remaining and you know that some of those years must be transitional. When one is coming up to a particular event, there are happenings that precede it and happenings afterwards. With your Earth it is the "proceeding" of going into another dimension. Therefore, there must be times when some of humanity, if they cannot keep up with her, will make their transitions and go to Nirvana and live happily for a while before the souls' need to keep evolving sends them out once again.

We speak of Earth changes, Readers, not to frighten you, but to light them up for you—to bring them to your attention. I know they have been talked about so long—more than thirty years even. However, they will become more dramatic. There will be more loss of life, if you think of it in those terms. We just think of it as a soul making a transition.

Now is not the time, dear Readers, to go into denial and just think of this as *hooey*. Or, another term could be *la-la land*, or fantasy. This is not la-la land. This is for real. The changes must be made. The Elohim, as we have said, can stave off the Earth changes for just so long. Then, you see, there could come a time when holding back the changes would not be helpful to her. She must make her changes and move forward. She wishes to move forward.

If humanity cannot keep up with the changes, then there will be loss of life. You have been told to stock your shelves with food that has a long shelf life. Put it in one corner of your cupboards or in a box in a closet, as this Channel has done. She has a month's supply on hand and as she has said if she does not use it herself, she can give it to others.

There will be a great exodus from the west into Arizona, as the changes start happening on the west coast. Arizona will be inundated with people fleeing from danger. It will tax her resources greatly. However, if everybody is forewarned and they open their hearts and refrigerators, all will be well.

Readers, you must stay in the Light and stay out of fear. Stay in peace and joy. Bring humor into this. When your house is overflowing with people so that one almost has to take a ticket for the next meal-call, laugh about it and enjoy it. Know that you are doing your part to help. That is part of being of service, you see.

There will be what we call *Rainbow Cities* developed. These are Enlightenment Centers that will be greatly protected by an aura that looks like a rainbow overhead—an energy band that protects the people that come. And why would they come? They will come because they are seeking peace; they are seeking freedom;

18

they are seeking love. They are searching for a place where they can be and not be afraid.

These are Enlightenment Centers, and they will be established and financed by your Heavenly Father, some even from lotteries for those who deserve it. And they will fund these cities and the money will flow to them and they will flow the money outward and not go into greed or hoarding. Of course, they can use it personally. It is theirs. They can pay off debts and buy whatever their needs are. Some will need to buy new cars and new clothes, simply because they have not for a while.

If their car is no longer running they will buy a new car, but they will lean toward a hybrid car that will run from a battery. These cars could then be recharged. The ships could even provide electrical power for the batteries. They could even provide crystals that would generate the electricity.

All of this is your future, dear ones—four years. It seems like a science fiction tale for sure, for we are merely speaking of four years. All must come to pass. After 2012, of course there will be more changes and transitions. As we go toward the years 2015 and 2020 the transition will continue.

People will be *offered* a release, a relief if they wish to take it. People will be offered to board the ships and stay with us while Earth has her changes and all calms down. Our time is different from yours, you see. We have no time as you know it. Tuella in one of her books said that 15 minutes of Earth time could be eight hours in Galactic time. You see you could spend years on our ships and it would only be several months or so on Earth, while she cleanses her shores, cleanses the air to where it is more breathable.

The Japanese people have long gone around wearing masks, for they do not want to breathe the germs of others. They are quite used to wearing masks. People in America are not so apt to want to be seen wearing a mask. They are afraid that they would be laughed at. And yet there could come a time when people will wear masks when they venture outside, for the air will be heavy with ash from the volcanoes.

You see, Readers what many people do not realize is that you could have several Earth changes at once! There could be one volcano in the west going off and then another volcano could erupt several miles from that one. You could have two spewing at once. Alaska could be having earthquakes and then California could have its quakes. This is what is going to tax the Nation—everything happening at the same time.

You have a government organization called FEMA, which proved to be totally inadequate for the victims of the hurricanes Katrina and Rita. Would you be able to depend upon FEMA when the Earth is going through her transitions? It is quite doubtful. Do not put your hopes on the government and its structured programs, dear ones. Put your hopes on yourself. Trust yourself, your soul. Trust the God of your heart and trust your wisdom. Your body carries great wisdom; trust that and know that your soul is leading you. Listen to yourself; listen to your heart. The times will be what you call *rough*. There will be rough times, dear ones.

However, if you will but ask us, our ships will be only too happy to land and lift some of you off to a happier place while this transition continues. There are what we call our *ground crew*, our *emissaries* who will take you to safe areas that I have told you—the Rainbow Cities. Keep your ears unplugged. Be open to new ideas. We will put as

20

much information in this book as we possibly can, ever keeping in mind that we cannot put all the information in at once, for people would go into overwhelm, which they may do anyway.

So dear Readers, I will step back now and as that saying goes *hang in there!* Ashtar likes to use Earth's slang, so many times he remarks *you ain't seen nothing yet! Keep your eyes on the skies.*

I am but a shout away. Please call upon me. I AM Lady Nada.

(*Oh, thank you Lady, it was very informative.*) You are welcome, dear one, and you are probably more in tune with what can happen than most people. You see, the information that Tuella put out thirty years ago has been forgotten by people or they do not know where to find it. Those little booklets are probably out of print.

All right, dear one, you have heard from my—shall we call her my better half? (Well, I do not think she is the better half but she is obviously a wonderful half!) Type it up, dear one, and I will be with you tomorrow. (Thank you, Lord.) You are welcome.

Good morning, dearest one, I Am Yeshua. We finished up yesterday with my Lady Nada giving a segment for the Introduction. We have one more person whom I would like to have come forward and speak. Most likely we will be able to finish this segment up in this sitting and then go on and start Chapter I. So relax and get ready to hear the next speaker. (All right, thank you.)

Good morning to the Readers and to this Channel. I am delighted to be here and to be a part of this book. You do not know me, but I know many of you. I had written many books in my day also. I am known as **Tuella.** (*Oh,*

Tuella, I have just been reading your books!) Well, I don't think many people do any more these days. But I did have my following, didn't I? *(Yes you did!)*

Now why have I come this morning? Of course I would come. I am back on the ships after having made my transition. I am with the Ashtar Command and still working in service for the Father. My transition was simply that, stepping from one reality into the next and before I knew it I was on the ship with my beloved brothers and sisters. Actually, it was a grand reunion. It also helped to know that I did not have to go down again and to do battle with the forces of darkness.

Today we are introducing a new book similar to the ones that I wrote in my day. This Channel is known as Chako, and she has a perfect name to just use her name and not bother with the last name, as I did with Tuella — Tuella's books. These will be known eventually as Chako's books — something that she has held in her heart and has brought to fruition.

Readers, let's get serious now. The days are fast approaching and, as Lady Nada has said, there will come a time in your not too distant future where there will be great rumblings of the Earth. There was a volcano that erupted just recently in the Red Sea. It erupted with such force that there is not that much left of the island. Or, we will say that the island is not that inhabitable with the lava going down to the sea.

Those volcanoes that explode in various parts of the world are but precursors of what is to come. When volcanoes explode in distant places, they are meant to catch the attention of humanity and to bring to your attention to not become complacent. This could happen in your back yard. Those of you on the west coast especially have very volatile backyards.

While Arizona is known for its summer heat, it is also known for its sacred spots in and around Sedona. This state will be a refuge for many, and the state will be hard pressed to know what to do with all of the refugees—and we will call them that.

When I say *we*, it is because we are never alone. One could say Tuella and her entourage, Lady Nada and her entourage, Yeshua and his entourage. We are never alone. Actually, Ashtar has millions in his entourage. However, in that crowd there is usually one dominant figure. At this point it is I, Tuella.

Therefore, dear Readers, see if you can find my past books. Many people of the older generation have them in their small archives. You see, much of what I described— those great Beings described things to me and then I wrote—much of that is very similar to what will be happening today, this present time, in this period of four years to 2012 and beyond. We are not crying *wolf*. We are offering you an opportunity to be lifted up to enjoy Earth's fireworks from above where you are safe. There are huge viewing screens where you can watch the volcanoes in action.

We are offering you this opportunity. We cannot force it upon you. There would be a wide spread panic if you felt that there was a mass evacuation and that you were forced to leave. NO, hear this! That would be against your free will. It is your free will that got you into this mess to begin with! The Earth was doing just fine evolving on her own until the dark decided to be greedy about it—to make wars with each other so that they could have more of what the others possessed. It is one of the Commandments in your Bible. ***Do not covet...***

People of power covet more power. They covet other countries' resources. They covet without one thought about their own evolution—about why they were born in America versus Iraq. It is as if they are not satisfied. They want to be safely in America but then they want in a greed-like manner to have Iraq's and Arabia's oils.

They do not realize that they were born into America for a specific karmic reason. Maybe it was to clean up their karma. Or they were born into a specific country so they could help humanity. But how many of you have seen political leaders actually helping? They are from long ago, the Reptilians, the dark, the Illuminati, and they are not about to give up that power. They may be male or female with a pretty face and brilliant mind. Of course Lizards are very wise. However, that does not give them the pure heart of Christ Consciousness. They can profess to love God but then do not serve Him in the Light.

People of Earth, you have doomed yourselves in many respects. Now I know there will be Readers who do not like that word *doomed*. But what I am talking about is the mentality of people—their karma—and how they have brought darkness to themselves. Would that not be your personal doomsday?

Earth herself is going on her merry way. She is reaching upward and she will evolve. However, she must be re-calibrated. Her axis is off. The days of the calendar are off. The calendar itself is off. Everything has gotten off track by humanity's darker thoughts and the pillaging of her resources—the killings of her forests and animals. Can you imagine killing one of those magnificent Indian tigers and putting him on your den wall? We here on the ships abhor to see that.

I have gotten off the subject a bit here, but you can see what my passion is. When I was on your Earth, I worked feverishly in service to the Father, writing the books, anchoring the New Jerusalem, which was actually my finest hour. Therefore, Readers, just know that what you have read in my books about the evacuation is no longer applicable in those terms.

However, it is being offered to you. Do you not see what a gift that is? What a gift that is by the Father—to give you dispensation for your karma and to bring you aboard the ships where the Christ Consciousness and frequencies are so high and pure with love. It might seem to a small child similar to being in a candy store. There is so much to choose from, so much to be delighted from, so much to be tasted. Oh, people, if you only could open your hearts and know the delights we have awaiting you.

And yes, after the Earth has settled down, we will bring you back down. You are not leaving forever. How would you like to come back to greener pastures where the water is pure, the air is pure, and once again the birds sing? The animals will roam freely and everything will be green. Where there is supposed to be a natural desert it will bloom in the springtime with the spring flowers.

People, realize from your hearts what a gift is being given to you. You are not being forced. You are not being evacuated from a fear-based decision. These are gifts we are offering you. Cannot you see what a gift it would be to you to see the Radiant One's ship land and to see him on your television sets and hear him on your radios? Perhaps if you were in the vicinity of where he is going to land, you

25

would feel that energy and see him in person—a band of love.

Therefore, what I am suggesting is not to be too quick in saying *no thanks*, for you are being given an opportunity of your lifetime. Accept it; walk with it with joy and love and anticipation, for it will be quite wonderful.

That is all I came to say. I am Tuella, a long past author.

(Oh, Tuella thank you so much. I just love your books. I just eat them up!) I see that you do and I see that you are reading one right now—as you did 27 years ago. But much of the material is still apropos. Bless you for wanting to read the words from the different Masters that came forth. Bless you. *(Thank you, Tuella.)*

Well, dear one, we thought that would be a treat for you. (It was wonderful. Goodness sake, she is a powerful lady.) That she is. So I will make a little closing statement now to this introductory chapter.

Readers, I hope we have sparked your imagination enough so that you will wish to continue reading the book, for we have much information that may be of interest to you. There will be times, when you are apt to say but I have read this before; or I have heard of that before. *And yes, you have and it is time to hear it again! So we will close this introductory chapter and go on to the next.*

This book will be set up in similar fashion as the previous ones. Each speaker will have his or her own chapter, so turn the page, and let us continue. 10-01-07

CHAPTER 1- ANDROMEDA REX

Good morning, Readers, I am one of the Presenters for this book. Again my name is Andromeda Rex. I will be speaking to you about the events to come. This is the year 2007 that is drawing to a close. However, it is so close to 2008, I will be speaking as if it were already 2008, with only four more years before it is 2012.

You may be wondering why there is a feeling of anticipation, as if, as the saying goes, *something is coming down*. Everything seems to be moving faster, but what you are feeling is that the Earth herself is somewhat off kilter. Now she is not going to flip or turn over or anything so dramatic. Those were indications of long ago. We have been able to stabilize her somewhat. However, her axis is a bit off and that will need to be straightened. It is being done gradually.

The year 2012 is not a cutoff date. There will be a blending. It is not just the time when one can say *OK, all the changes are completed. It is done.* Energy does not work like that. Energy moves from one object to another. The Earth is transiting from one dimension to another. In order to do this, she is cleansing one part of herself and then another part. She is doing this by releasing pressure through her volcanoes and through her earthquakes from all the different faults that line the planet.

Since this channel lives in Arizona, we will speak mostly about America. There are major fault lines criss-crossing this country. Some are deeper than others. People do not realize that epicenters can be deep in the Earth.

However, there is always a warning. Mother Earth gives a warning. Nature gives a warning. Birds stop flying. Household pets become very nervous. Animals seek higher ground. It is as if the world listens. It is similar to being in the eye of a hurricane. Everything stills. The winds still. Everything is in anticipation for a mountain to blow or for the crust of the Earth to break open. This will happen, dear people. It may happen where you are. Maybe you were meant to be there. Maybe this is where you will make your own transition. Or, maybe you are there to help others. Keep in mind that when people are in what might be called dangerous areas, many times they are there not to die, but to help others in need in order to help *them* from dying. That could be the karmic reason, you see.

People want to know the timetable. We can only say that there can be no timetable. It is similar to asking someone when is he going to regurgitate. He does not know. He just feels sick. When is it actually going to happen, he does not know. He can be giving loud belches which is what the volcanoes do. The earthquakes can rumble. The oceans can become more powerful in their breakers. The tides may change, but no one knows when the quake will happen or when the giant tsunami is going to come.

We can only offer you an avenue of escape, dear people. Our ships can land and remove you if you will but ask. There will be an increase in telepathy, for that is one of the major ways to communicate — mental telepathy. You may wonder how are you going to tell us that you want to be lifted up onto a ship. We reply that you *think* it; you send us the message telepathically. We hear you. We have those of you who are our Emissaries and Lightworkers pinpointed on our great computers. We hear your thoughts and they are registered on the computers. They make a note of what you are thinking, speaking, or reading. It is noted when the thought is of the Light. Consequently, we can check the computers, for they keep track of the person's energy field. When someone is praying and talking to God and thinking about spiritual things, that is all registered. We hear you and we can see you. Therefore, do not hesitate and think that your call for help will be ignored, for it has been registered already on our computers.

The day will come when your call for help will be answered. Some of you already know this. Some of you will be ready. And some of you will need to be guided to those Rainbow Cities that Lady Nada told you about. In those cities, your vibratory rate can be increased so that you can be lifted aboard safely, if you so choose.

We are thinking only of a rate of 200, Readers. That is not that high a number. All of humanity can reach that number if they choose to. It takes, of course, right thinking, holding your thoughts of Light. It takes being in your heart, feeling love, and being love. It takes willingness to be of service and to help others. It takes correct foods. Some can eat meat and others cannot. Some can eat raw foods and others cannot.

Each body is different. Age enters in. If an elderly body has eaten a certain way most of its life, changing its diet could be more destructive than a blessing. As Ashtar has said, age is not a yardstick for being beamed aboard. We have many ways to lift you aboard. We could land and you could walk aboard. We can take your etheric body and bring you aboard. We can take you during your sleep. You would just wake up in a different bed. And there will be angels with you all the time who will calm you.

This is not something to fear. This is a blessing that is being given to you. I will close for now and will pick up where I left off at a later time. I AM Andromeda Rex.

Good morning, our dearest one, I was listening while you were talking to the Father and expressing your grief for humanity that does not know that our ships are of the spiritual quality. They do not know that yes, the Spiritual Hierarchy travels around in spaceships. It seems too awesome for them. They can think of me as trodding the Earth while in Israel. Some can think of me as trodding the Earth in India. But to think that in fact I may have my own spaceship, that is too much of a stretch for humanity.

This is where your books and others are helping to bring people into the 21st century—to let them know that your Space Brothers and Space Sisters are just as much of the Spiritual Hierarchy, the Spiritual Planes of the Father as anything else they have in their mind. It is a hard concept for people, isn't? (Yes.)

All right, dear one, we are in the midst of Chapter I and I understand that Heather, our devoted editor, has done her usual fine job with the Introductory chapter and pronounced it excellent. *That is what we like to hear. Thank you, Heather, for your vote of confidence (chuckles).*

Now let's get serious, as Tuella said (still chuckling). I will step aside here so that Andromeda Rex can continue.

Good morning once again to our dear Channel. I **AM Andromeda Rex,** back once again to continue our chapter. I am honored to be the one to more or less open the book, shall we say. As Yeshua has said, this book is to

30

help bring people forward. There are so many of them who have not read Tuella or the other modern day prophets who told what one could expect with the different Earth changes. So we are saying it again for everyone, bringing you up to date.

Now in the next few years, and when I say *few*, I am speaking of the few years leading up to 2012 and perhaps beyond, people will have decisions to make. People will have decisions as to relocating. Are they feeling that where they are is no longer safe? This might be people on the west coast, perhaps, if they are too close to the ocean or near the major fault lines, or near sleeping volcanoes.

The people may be feeling *antsy*. They just cannot settle down. They cannot quite put words to their feelings. They no longer are really happy where they are. They may have beautiful homes and a beautiful view. However, it no longer brings joy to them. They are being guided by their souls. Their souls are saying that it is time to move and build a new life some place else. Now it does not have to be in Arizona or Colorado. They may have relatives elsewhere whom they can visit to see if that is where they would like to settle.

Many people on the west coast are getting the message that it is time to move. Some people have their houses up for sale and are having a hard time selling them, simply because of the down-turn in the housing market. That will turn around, but not for a while—maybe not even in the rest of this year, or going into 2008. However, it will turn around.

It will turn around, you see, when the Earth changes start on the west coast, for then the housing industry will

31

boom again for those who are not in those western states. There will be more houses built in Arizona, Colorado, Nevada, and Utah. People will have the urge to move.

It might be a little-known fact for those of you who are not into New Age Thought that there is a term we use to describe bodies: *solid*. We say that a body is more solid, which means that there is not a great percentage of Light in the body, versus those whose bodies are of the higher consciousness.

In those more solid bodies, it makes no difference if their soul is trying to guide them. The personality-ego does not feel it. The personality overrides any guidance. Those types of people are slow to change. They like their way of life, especially if they are seniors. They can become stuck in their ways; they slow down and the thought of having to move and get away to a new area is not appealing to them. Therefore, they procrastinate. One could say that the next few years could be ones of procrastination! People know they must make a change but are not willing to do it; so they keep putting it off and putting it off. They do not listen to their own soul. Their will-ego overrides their own soul. These people then have a difficult time. They are not even sitting on a fence with the decision to go one way or the other, they are just mired down and stuck.

Some of them read books, but they are apt to read detective stories. They are not so apt to read science-fiction or books that are of the New Age Thought, such as our books. Our books travel by word-of-mouth. They get passed around. People send for them by e-mail and then the Author guides them to Trafford, her publisher. This present book will fan out further than the last one. It seems as if each book she writes has a wider distribution of readers.

Therefore, you have these people who refuse to change and are not listening to their own guidance. And before you know it, they are the ones who are trying to get their cars out of sink holes, or are fleeing from mud slides, or even fleeing from forest fires—anything that is of nature. They are not in a safe spot and were not listening to the guidance that they were receiving to be at the right place at the right time.

Our ships have most of the Lightworkers pinpointed. We watch over you. We monitor the Earth. Some people are apt to become alarmed when they think that they are being watched, for they take it that we are also watching their private moments. It does not work that way. The computer registers your thoughts and your reading material and your communications to others. It is set up to more or less sound an alarm when your body is in a dangerous situation.

These safety features are programmed as part of the computer—written in. Keep in mind that the computers do not see a full physical body. If you sleep nude, it is only noted that there is no body covering. There is not an exact picture of what you look like. It is difficult to describe, but could be similar to looking at a negative or an x-ray. The computers do not see things considered private by humanity, knowing that there are private moments— intimacy in relationships, personal hygiene. Do not become anxious, for we are not voyeurs (*chuckles*).

Again, when all of this will take place is in the hands of God. We have set up different scenarios so that we would have every contingency under consideration. Say that something happens in one way. We have that contingency covered so that we can help. If it does not play out like we thought, we have it covered in the next scenario and the next and next one. For example, there are just so many ways one can fall into a river. We have just so many ways that we can rescue you. Consequently, it is noted where Lightworkers are in unsafe areas versus other people. They are more or less red-flagged, so that we will know this.

If people live near bodies of water, we know that that could become a hazard. If people live where there is a great deal of snow, we know that, for that could become a hazard. We know those who are living on fault lines, for that could become a hazard. This Channel has recently read that there is a giant fault line that runs from the Seattle area to the Appalachians. This could definitely become a hazard for those thousands living along that fault!

What humanity does not realize is that we have the capacity to react instantly. In your finite mind, you think that an alarm bell or a siren must go off. We have light flashes and color changes. If for any reason a person needed to be rescued, we can do so.

However, people need to give us permission. It would behoove people to set it up ahead of time, simply by prayer, and asking the Father. Therefore, if for any reason a situation develops where their body would be in extreme life or death danger because of nature's cleansing and the chances are that death would come before its time, a ship could lift them up for those few minutes and bring them back down. This we can do. We can bring you up in seconds and bring you back down. You might not know you have been lifted, for it can happen instantly.

There are strange stories of how people had escaped a major disaster but do not know how they did it. They just find themselves dazed and somewhat dusty, not having realized they were taken up briefly and brought back down again. You have heard so many times that *there are no accidents,* and that is literally true. Therefore, if a disaster is headed your way and it is not karmic and you have not listened to your soul to get out of the way, you can have it already on record—*please Father, help me in case I am coming into horrendous danger; help me in whatever way in your wisdom is correct for me.* Set it up!

You have heard so many times that your prayers are answered, so set it up ahead of time. I imagine you have never thought of that. *Do you mean that I can pray ahead of time to ask to be beamed up if the going gets too rough for me?* Yes, you can if it is not a karmic situation. You can just know in your heart that you will be in the right place at the right time. However, if for some reason it has become impossible for you, then you can be lifted up and then at some later time be brought back down.

Think of all the mothers who could be giving birth at the time of a tsunami, a hurricane, or an earthquake, whether at home, in hospitals or in a car. We can lift them up and bring them back down with a newborn in their arms **if** they have set it up ahead of time. All they need to do is ask. All we need is to have it on our records. She acknowledges us and has asked for our help. Then we can step in because it has become her free will instruction.

35

ANDROMEDA REX

There are some people who want to experience some of the Earth changes. They want to know what is it like when a volcano goes off and to be able to see the awesome display. They want to know what it feels like to be in a major earthquake, as long as it does not kill them, that is. However, the danger to them is if they wait too long or cut it too close. That is when we can step in if they had given us previous permission. Or if there is time, they could even yell from where they are for us to come to them. We have millions of ships guarding the planet at this time, waiting to see if and when we will be needed.

I think that is all I need to say for this chapter—the main theme being that you can set it up ahead of time to be lifted aboard the ship for your safety's sake and then be beamed down when it is safe once again. All we need is your permission. And if you hold love in your heart and are not afraid of us, that will help also. Even if you do not vibrate at that 200 frequency, the love will help neutralize the beam's strength.

With that, Readers, I will bless you now and perhaps speak to you again at the end of our book. I AM Andromeda Rex.

(Thank you and sir, would you please state your official position or title, for so many people have not heard of you?)

I am from that cluster of stars *Andromeda*. I carry that energy. I help Ashtar on the ship. I can wear several hats, one could say, but it is always to assist him in any way that I can to help monitor Earth—basically, to be his right-hand man, and this I do gladly. *(Thank you.)* You are welcome. 10-04-07

CHAPTER 2- YESHUA

Good morning dearest Readers and to this Channel, **I AM Yeshua,** *back for another sitting and an exciting new chapter. This is our second chapter, and you have caught on to the theme, I see. (Yes, Lord, chuckles.) We felt it was about time that humanity knew that yes, the* <u>Spiritual Hierarchy</u> <u>has</u> <u>its</u> <u>own</u> <u>spaceships</u>*! You can put that in staccato-type print. We have our own ships. I guess I will not stretch it too far and say that Aspects of God have Their own ship also.*

Now who are we bringing in today for this second chapter? I wish to go back a little to the early 1980's where much was being given out and written about the coming possible evacuations and the Earth changes that would make it so. As you know, this has not come to pass. It was approximately thirty years ago that we were quite worried, for the Earth was in imminent danger of rolling, turning over—just like you turn over in your bed. She was very close to that. We had to bring in millions of ships to help stabilize her.

The Elohim were working furiously to stave off this disaster. Since many of you are still alive from that era, you know that we were able to do so. Now it is coming up to being very close to the deadline of 2012. It is a date that has been set into motion—an historical date that brings to prophecy much that has been written.

However, will it be as dangerous as first portrayed by the different prophecies of the Mayan calendar, Hopi Indians, our modern prophets such as Gordon-Michael

Scallion, the authors of the I AM America books and many, many others? All of that information for you former Readers, present Readers, and future Readers has been somewhat neutralized. California is not going to break off and sink. However, there will be parts of that state that will be in dire straits, and those are the parts that are nearest to the ocean. Do I dare say that the famous Malibu shores will be no more? Actually, they will be displaced and could be a hundred miles or so further inland.

What does that mean? It means that parts of southern California could be under the sea. You have been warned about this before, Californians. Listen to your souls. They are guiding you. It is interesting to note that many of the famous movie stars do not live there, but in other parts of the country like North Dakota, Idaho, Colorado and on the east coast. You need to be aware, Readers, that not all of the past information will be negated. Those of you who have kept the old material, get it out and re-read it, for there is much truth there.

Much has been written recently about what is known as **Stasis**, *when the Earth could be put into a sleeping mode, a homeostasis, an animated suspension. These are all terms that describe what possibly could occur. Whether it does or not depends on the thought forms of humanity. Can you change your thoughts so you are centered on love and peace versus darkness and war? The purpose of the Stasis idea was to allow time for the benevolent Space Command to work upon Earth without being hindered by guns and tanks of war.*

There is much that we could adjust with our energies and technology, but humanity does not let us get close enough to help you! This we could do if people were taking a long, Rip van Winkle-type of nap (chuckles). Now I know this scares many people. This is not a probability yet, but it is a strong possibility. It is always dubious to try to put timetables to these ideas that are so "out there," shall we say. People cannot make that adjustment—that leap of thought when something is too outrageous. The thought of putting the whole Earth into a deep sleep for three weeks is in that category, I must admit.

However, remember that many times there are facts within the fiction. There are facts within this proposal which may come into fruition. This book is to wake people up and, hopefully, not put them to sleep (chuckles). We attempt to give you as much information as we possibly can.

It is similar to a "heads-up" call—take note of this; watch out for this. This is a strong possibility. That is what we are doing. We are giving you wake-up calls. Do not become so complacent and think that your lives will continue on an even keel. They will not. No one is living on an even keel these days. There is so much that is changing with the new energy that is coming onto the planet. Every eclipse, every full moon brings these energy changes to humanity. In the last chapter Andromeda Rex described how bodies can be solid and not feel that much so that very possibly people do not realize they are being bombarded by these new energies until they become ill.

Those who have bodies that carry more Light in them are having strange effects. They are experiencing things with their bodies that do not make sense to them. Why does the sun bring such strong rays that it can cause severe rashes on the skin? These rashes do not itch, but are under the skin like red freckles and blotches, whether it is covered or not. You can have on long trousers and sandals, but the red freckles go all the way to the knees. Just walking to the mailbox in the strong Arizona sun can bring it on, especially if your feet are in sandals where the skin is exposed. Wearing a sunblock lotion may help some people, but it does little for others. Energies are bombarding the body and creating different effects on the body.

This we note. We can see this on our computers. You have been told how we watch over you and how you are pin-pointed on our screens, We watch the changes that come over your body. That is part of our job descriptions—to watch how the different energies are affecting the body. How can or do the bodies adjust? We watch for this and see if the rashes disappear when a body is not exposed to the sun for a few weeks. We will know then that the body can adjust. Will it happen each time? That remains to be seen. These different energies coming forward have a great deal to do with the physical conditions of the bodies on Earth.

To get back to what is referred to as Stasis, *the percentage of its happening is debatable, but the chance is still there. On a scale of 1-10, it probably is a 6-7. It could happen; it could happen.*

Now, I have sort of taken over this second chapter, so I think I will continue and make it my chapter. In case you have forgotten who has been speaking...

I AM Yeshua. I was telling you that much information that was put out over thirty years ago can be brought forward again. Some of it will happen and some of it will not. Those of you who have the older books in your archives, take them out and read them, as this Channel has done. There will be times when much of that information could be true once again, but to a lesser degree.

Does it not make sense to you to store up some water, to have some gallon jugs of water stashed away? Does it not make sense to you to have a month's supply of food stashed away? Does it not make sense to you to have a flashlight that does not require batteries, or if it does require batteries to have several on hand? You have all been in those violent storms where your houses have lost power and you are left in the dark trying to find a candle and matches in order to bring in some light.

Therefore, could it not be in your reality to know that there could be electrical storms generated from some of the Earth changes? There could be times when there is no rain but electric strikes one after the other—lightening flashing all over the sky. I hope none of you have metal flag poles near your home, for they are like lightening rods. In fact this Channel was living in a townhouse complex in Minnesota that had a metal flagpole in the front of the common area. Lightening struck the pole, traveled underground and blew out the phone boxes for several houses away, including this Channel's house. So you see how electricity can travel. Many a golfer has found this out—standing under a tree during a storm and wearing metal cleats on his/her shoes. Therefore, be aware that there will be electrical storms during the cleansing.

Now I mentioned the food supply. The reason was because stores may not be receiving their shipments of food. A great deal of food comes from the coastal areas which may be inundated by the high waters from tidal waves. With the displaced people coming in from the

41

coasts, the grocery stores' shelves could be depleted in a short period of time. Those of you with your month's supply of food will not panic. You will also be able to feed some of the people whom you will be housing in your homes. You see it is wise to listen, be cautious, and be prepared and then you can forget about it. Would it not be more advantageous to have your month's supply of food stashed away some place versus being in a panic as to what to eat? Some people may only have dry cereal to eat. Why does that have to be—if they only had listened and prepared. I am not the only one saying this. This has been said before to other spiritual groups in other states. People who read what is known as New Age material have long heard of this. Many of them have become complacent and have not followed the suggestions; so it is being offered again.

Therefore, we are saying to have your extra water, food, and flashlights, and all will be well. If you wanted to go ahead and buy the masks that one can wear over your nose for when the volcanic ash makes it difficult to breathe, that could be helpful too. There could come a time when the majority of the people in the United States will be wearing masks when they venture outdoors. They would be wise to do so and not be worried so much about the cosmetic effect but to have some of the pollutants strained out of the air that they are breathing in.

Now I have talked about that. Let us continue and talk about the housing situation. How many of you are living where it is safe? How many of you are living where the house is huge with many square feet? How are you going to heat that house, or cool it? Or are you planning to fill the house with refugees, whether family or distant relatives or humanity's family? Give situations like this some thought. That is what this book is about—to make you think, to make you prepare. That is the book's purpose—to bring you up to date.

There has not been that much written about evacuations lately. In order to bring you up to date, we say that evacuations are fear-based. We prefer to call them lift-offs, and these are being offered to you on a first-come first-served basis. They are suggestions. They are our gift. Remember back to when Katrina and Rita were wreaking havoc on the Gulf states with the hurricane winds and the water inundation. Would not those people who were sitting on their roof-tops waiting for a helicopter to rescue them have been relieved and in much joy to be lifted aboard a loving ship in the sky—a ship where there is water to bathe in, clean clothes to put on, abundant food and a warm bed and the feeling of peace and joy and fellowship? Would those people not have embraced that opportunity?

What did they get instead? They got lifted or bused to a dome that had sanitation overflowing, no means of privacy, little to no food and much chaos amidst the wailing sounds of the babies. This is what we are saying, dear friends: the lift-offs that we are offering are ones of joy, to take you temporarily to a safer place on the ships. That is why we are calling it a lift-off versus an evacuation, for it will be *your* choice and not a command. We are definitely allowing your free will. Hear this: **there will be no mass evacuation**, for that signifies that people are brought aboard against their will. This is not to be.

Be as children. Children will view this as being a grand adventure—going to Disney Land in the sky with the adventures awaiting them, food awaiting them. We even have entertainment for the younger people. Therefore, it

43

would not be so much different as they knew on Earth, except if they were poor and living in poverty conditions with little to eat, they will find that none of that exists on the ships. All they need to do is ask; give us a sign that gives us their permission.

Many people have read the books put out by Lady Tuella and others. There were definite guidelines and timelines as to where to go and what to expect, what to bring or what not to bring; how they were going to be beamed up or walked aboard. We are not following such strict instructions this time, for we are coming to offer help and allowing it to be your choice.

How many of you have gone to those areas that were devastated by fierce storms and asked the survivors if you could help them in any way? They gladly said *oh, if you could bring us some water or some food.* Or *oh, I cannot find my baby. Would you help me find my child?* They are asking for help, and this we will provide gladly and lovingly.

Those who were in poverty will experience it no more. I also want to stress that one's station in life will make no difference as to who will be beamed aboard. It is the love in your heart and your giving us your permission. *Rich man, poor man, beggar-man, thief, doctor, lawyer, merchant, Chief*—all are welcomed aboard if they but ask. Their stations in life are equal in our eyes, for it is the soul of those Beings that we look at, not the personality.

The soul of a beggar could be on a higher plane than the soul of the rich man. Both souls are *working their karma*, as the saying goes. Those with heart and a true belief of being in service to God will have no problem

44

being beamed aboard. Others could drop their bodies on the way. Therefore, we will not take those but we will lead them to those Rainbow Cities that we have described to you before where their frequencies can be raised.

There are so many different scenarios that could be played out, but we think we have thought about all of them. However, even we could be surprised as to what could play out. But dearest Readers, we have only your best interests at heart. We do not want to control you in any way. We do not want to take away your free will. We will stand back until you ask us to come forward and help you. And then you will be flooded with so much help that you will wonder why you had not asked for help before.

The lift-off will happen in a blinking of your eyes and you will be aboard ship. It will feel like it is an abundant fairyland, a dream, a candy store for the children, a church, a university for those scholars, but in actuality it would be just our Ships of Light. This is who we are; this is how we live, and this is how we react.

With that, dearest Readers, I will bring Chapter 2 to a close. May you read it with an open mind and an opened heart and a willingness to change—a willingness to see an opportunity that is being given to you. Willingness, love and peace with no fear is all that is required of you.

I bless you, my dearest ones. I AM Yeshua.

Your Space Brothers and Sisters Greet You

CHAPTER 3- ASHTAR' S COMMENTS

Good morning, dearest one and to our Readers. I AM Yeshua, back once again to continue our book. I hope you Readers have made it this far, for it may be quite provocative for those of you who carry no concept of spaceships being benevolent and being on your side of the fence—the fence of love, peace, harmony, and devotion to the Father. Our ships, dear souls, are on your side. Embrace us as we come forward with offerings of help and technology.

What a wonderful place Earth will be indeed, when we are able to land and people are excited to see us and we are excited to be among you. That is our dream; that is our hope.

This morning I will bring back one of the previous Presenters, for there is more that he wishes to talk about, to present to you and to tell you about. Therefore, I will step back now and let him speak.

Good morning, Readers, this is **Ashtar** once again. Since we are talking about the ships, we are obviously speaking about the Ashtar Command—a Command that is full of Light and love, a Command for the purpose of helping Earth readjust to the transition that she will make. Be at peace, Readers; be at peace, for that is how we come.

This book is to give you new ideas and to awaken you to the fact that yes, perhaps there are spaceships and perhaps they are not all of the dark. No dark ships are allowed in the Earth's atmosphere. At one time there were

47

but no longer. That period of many years ago is past. The Grays will not be landing to experiment on you—to see how your parts work, to flip your arms and to watch you walk and to see how you reproduce. That is not appropriate and that is not allowed.

Therefore, do not give it a second thought. No ship but ours of peace will come to your shores. They cannot get through the shield we have put around Earth. We have millions of ships of the benevolent nature that belong to the Federation of Galactic Light. These ships monitor your Earth and also act as a barrier to any other ships that may want to come out of curiosity. However, they are not allowed. There is a ring-pass-not; we created a ring-pass-not through which those of the dark cannot pass.

My particular ship is called the *Phoenix*, as in the Phoenix bird that rises out of the ashes into the Light. And we are forever rising upward into the Light of God, joining hands with the Radiant One, Lord Sananda Kumara, Esu. He is known throughout the Universes for the radiant Light that he carries.

We will be approaching different people, those we have designated as our ground crew, or our Emissaries. We have in one way or another been in contact with them. We may have personally brought them aboard during their lifetime; or we may have connected with them through a spiritual reading that they have received. We are forever seeking those Lightworkers. We have many that we come through, for they are a direct channel for us and we can come through them with our Essence.

For this Channel, we come into her heart and telepathically speak to her. She is a dedicated soul and it is her destiny, as we have told her. It is her destiny to work for us and with us until we can say *it is finished*. She is not the only one, of course. There are thousands and thousands throughout the planet.

We have ships over the houses of these special Emissaries. Some have seen us, while others have not. Where there are specific groups that meet and speak of us and send us loving thoughts, we have a ship over the churches where they meet. You will be surprised, for there is not much that gets beyond us, for our technology is so advanced that it can pick up the energies and thoughts of people.

It will be important during these next several years for people to have cleared themselves. People who are on the path work with their bodies throughout the years. Psychotherapists and teachers are forever talking about the importance of clearing oneself. There are many categories in that. One could almost think of it as a *clearance rack*. On that rack you put your past lives that no longer serve you. You put your grievances that no longer serve you. You put your ambitions and anything that you have coveted, for you are clearing yourself so that more Light can occupy your many shelves.

Your bodies are great holding closets. The cells hold all of the memories of the past. Those memories need to be brought forward and sorted and released. You can also think of it as walking a path and consciously side-stepping a fallen tree branch, or side-stepping weeds, rocks and boulders in order to get to the clear path—the path that is of golden Light.

It has been discussed with this Channel whether we of the spaceships are as spiritual as the Spiritual Hierarchy. In fact there have been people who questioned whether the Spiritual Hierarchy is associated with spaceships. Let me reiterate that the **Radiant One is our Commander-in-Chief of the ships—Sananda.** One cannot get more spiritual than that to be under his Command! We have meditation rooms, or what you'd call *chapels* on our ships. We literally can go and speak with God. We are of the Light. We are in Light bodies so bright that you could not see us or be able to keep your eyes opened as you looked at us.

You see, many times when people are trying to designate who is spiritual and who is religious, they put it in a biblical sense, simply because they know no other way to differentiate, to speculate, to visualize. They have been programmed so much throughout the years with religiosity and do not have a clear demarcation between what is spiritual and what is religious. Your religious leaders would say that it must be from the Bible where every word is true. Or it must be from the Cross experience. Or it must be from the resurrection and ascension.

The problem lies in the fact that some of that is true and some of it is not. As we have said before, your dear Jesus did not die on the cross. Yet so much of your Christian religion is based on their supposed facts that he died on the cross. Well, he was not on the cross and therefore, could not have died on it. (Book FOUR from this Channel tells about all of this, so that I do not have to go into it again. *Realities of the Crucifixion.*)

However, that is religion. But what about spirituality? Spirituality is the Light of Christ

Consciousness. Spirituality is being of service, love of God, but allowing those great biblical personages to live in the correct way—the spiritual way and not the religious way. Some people may say *well that is how* you *see it, but I see it differently.* So again, there is a difference between spirituality and religiosity.

We of the Space Command are not religious in any way, but we are totally spiritual. We rub shoulders and walk arm in arm with the Radiant One, that Son of God, that man of heart beyond description. Readers, just know that we too are Light and love and peace and we have your best interests at heart.

There has been so much written about what these next several years will be like. People write of the Earth changes and the disasters. Thirty or forty years ago we proposed evacuation. However, we are bringing you up to date. It is 2007 as I speak and in three months it will be 2008. Sometimes as I think about what I can say, I am struck by the awesome, awesome task that we of the Galactic Ashtar Command have taken on. It is a task that was given to us by the Father.

This is His planet. This is His creation, His dream to make a planet of no duality, but to have Heaven on Earth where people can live in peace and love and harmony— where there is a balance with Nature and the animals can frollick in freedom once again without being afraid. Nature also is involved, for it is she who will create and bring the elements together in order for the various changes to take place.

Picture an island in the Pacific Ocean where the population is small and the people are free-spirited souls.

51

Picture that island being decimated by the force of a hurricane and the inundation of water to the point where the island is no more. This will happen. The maps that are drawn of the world will need to be greatly revised in the following years, for in many places there will no longer be land. In other areas there will be land that has risen from the oceans and had not been visible before—the rising and falling of Earth.

However, what can one expect in America? There will be incidences of tidal waves where those on the west coast could lose their back porch, as the giant waves claw at the sandy cliffs. The coasts are very vulnerable— California, Florida, Boston and New York are especially vulnerable. The area around Seattle, Washington, is very vulnerable. This is when people need to listen to their guidance and move when it is necessary.

We are offering you a way out. People may accept it or they may not, for it is a gift to you. If you have given us your permission, we can rescue you and give you a respite from the worries of trying to keep your body safe. Let go of your possessions and come aboard where all of your needs will be met and then some. It will seem like a fairy tale to you. Your wish is but our command.

This is all that I wanted to say—a short chapter, but lots of food for thought. Call this chapter, *Ashtar's Comments*. That is all, dear Readers; that is all. (*Thank you, Ashtar.*) You are welcome. Keep your eyes on the skies!

All right, dear one, are you ready for another one? (Yes, I think so.) Then let us bring back Tuella. (I will make hers a separate chapter, Readers, so please turn the page.)

CHAPTER 4- LADY TUELLA SPEAKS

Good morning Readers, I am back once again. **I AM Tuella.** When I walked your planet, I wrote several books about the Space Command and used my name of Tuella. Now I am a Lady Master and aboard the sacred ships. Those of you who have read my books will know they were mainly about coming evacuations. That is no longer to be. Things have changed and the Ashtar Command is more proficient at what it can do.

I wonder if you have thought of that—everything changes and so does the Command. The technology that the Command had years ago is not as advanced as it is today. They are able to do more things. They are able to lift you in the twinkling of an eye if it is your wish.

When I walked your Earth, there was a growing interest in spaceships. However, people mixed it up in their heads. They associated the ships with being brought aboard against their will and being experimented upon. Then that movie *Strange Encounters* came out which showed a Mothership landing.

Even I did not know how magnificent these ships are until after I had made my transition. I do not have the vocabulary to give it to you now, because it is not in your reality yet. If a rose is a different color that you have never seen, how could I give you the color when there is no vocabulary for it? What these ships can do now is out of your pictures of reality. You simply could not fathom them yet.

However, I can tell you that if you make the choice to be lifted aboard it will fulfill your wildest dreams of fantasy. Everything will be given to you. You have no idea of the culinary arts that their cooks possess. Or how they can program computers to make it all happen—program the computer to prepare this magnificent banquet and push a button and let the banquet begin with all the foods ready on dishes of your design. Sheldan Nidle mentions this on his video *Landings 101* and it is true.

You will be able to sit at great screens and dial in any of your past lives that you wish to review. Or if you do not know what they are, you can scroll down and read the titles. You will have different names throughout your history. Most likely as you think back on your historical events, you will have had a life during that time. Whether it was peaceful or one that was war-like, you had come for that soul's experience, and you would be able to view that life.

You would be able to see where your Light body is stored for those of you who have your Light bodies stored in suspended animation. Those are for the more highly developed souls whose Light bodies await them. You come aboard and slip into them and remember little of what was on Earth. However, if you are supposed to remember, that will be given to you.

We do not wish to beam people aboard and have them forget what was going on on Earth, but to watch the Earth changes so that they will know why they are on board ship. Then they can watch the aftermath and how growth starts to happen with the vegetation and trees—air pure once again. There is so much to view, similar to walking through a fairy book, or childhood stories of Gulliver's

Travels. However, you would be on board ship and walking through them and re-living them if you wish.

On another side, you can take classes. You will have instructors who will teach you different languages. These languages can be programmed into your brain so that you learn them, speak them correctly and will know them. How would you like to speak French? You sit in the audio studios and have a teacher on a monitor that can see you. You have a one-on-one teacher and you are speaking. When you finish, you know the language. You may not have realized that you had just spent several months studying it on the ship, for in actuality it was only an hour or so of Earth time. This is how many people will learn English so that when they come back down, lifted down to Earth, they will know English.

We have a universal language of Light, but it is doubtful whether that will be taught as the predominant language. The Galactic Command has its own language and this you will be taught while you are on board ship. This you will learn in an effortless way.

If you have a particular skill that you wish to acquire and you always wanted to be someone that could design and make clothes—your couture clothes—you can take those lessons. You could design any garment that you wished and use our instruments to make it. You could make it within an hour's Earth time. Therefore, when you come back down you could be wearing a new suit of clothes also.

Therefore, dear Readers, I hope I have sparked your interest also. That is what this lift-off is all about. Take out any fear that you may have. We are offering you Alice in Wonderland on our space ships, truly a place of awe and things that you cannot even imagine that are beautiful, informative, instructive, for even when you are aboard, the soul needs to keep learning and growing. It will be a beautiful experience for you and one that you will cherish forever.

I AM Tuella.

CHAPTER 5- ANDROMEDA REX, ENCORE

Good morning, dearest one, I have been watching you struggle with your computer this morning and having a bit of trouble. (Once in a while, yes.) That will pass; that will pass. Now you have just finished transcribing Tuella's potent little chapter. The Readers who have not read her books of long ago will be surprised to read this information, for it will be new to them.

Now we are going to advance somewhat and bring in a deeper depth for this book. I am going to bring back one of the Presenters who has graciously consented to speak further. It is our comrade and dearest friend, Andromeda Rex. He is overseeing much of what is going on in the world. He will be a tremendous help for people, if they but will listen. I will step aside now.

Good morning once again. **I AM Andromeda Rex**. I was not expecting to come back again so soon, but there is information that your Lord wanted me to convey to all of you. As you know there has been great speculation as to whether the Earth was going to go into the Big Sleep—called *Stasis*—or not. That is still on hold!

You know when there is a group of souls such as we, and I am speaking of the highest Masters and God, we have round table discussions. We speak of many factors that are part of the dramatization that is going on on Earth. When we sit at a Council, all plans are laid on the table. We hold nothing secret. We hold nothing back, for we are coming together in love and partnership but at the same time allowing each other's ideas—allowing each other's criticisms that are given with love. Some of the Masters have levels of expertise that the others do not carry. We listen with respect, for that Master has earned that designation and he or she knows what he/she is talking about, and we respect that. Therefore, when the idea of Stasis was approached, we put it on the table. *Let's look at this; let's see if this is feasible and can work. What can it do that would be more conducive to helping Earth? What could it not do. Would it bring fear to people and hinder them from making reasonable, logical decisions?*

Many times we must consider where humanity is on the different levels of consciousness. Are people at a level where they can hear our reasons? Are they at a level of consciousness where they will understand that it is for their protection, for their advancement? Can they understand that? Of course we realize that not everyone is at the same level of consciousness. There are different strata on any world. Earth is not the only one. All worlds have different levels of awareness, and there is always the Grand Council. There is always the God of that world that guides the people and there is also the Supreme Father-Mother of all.

As we in our Councils looked at Earth, we could see what is lacking. There is little cohesiveness. You know, Readers, it is love that combines everyone. People may profess love and I believe it was Korton who spoke of love-communication, for people who love many times consider it to be a *possessive* energy versus an *allowing* energy. There is little allowing on your planet. The egos are strong. The dark energies are strong and much of humanity, although they profess a love of God, carry the dark side of themselves and have not cleared themselves, as we have said in the previous chapters. (*Review Chapter 3 by Ashtar.*)

58

Therefore, we look at Earth to determine how can we help her and still stay in the parameters of free will. Consequently, it was brought to the Council table. I am not going to specify which particular Master proposed *Stasis*, for when we join in Council, we are one and speak as one voice. In our Council that day, it was proposed that we put humanity into a deep sleep. We knew that this could bring fear to people when they found out about it. There would be those who would question whether we had taken their free will if we put them to sleep without their knowing it. Of course that is a valid question—a valid argument, which we also had pondered in our Council. *Would this be overstepping the souls' free will?*

However, at the same time then there was the argument *for* Stasis. The world is in dire need of balance. It is in dire need of raising her vibratory rate. It is in dire need of re-calibrating time as you know it, for it has gotten off track, we shall say. Your Earth's axis has wobbled off track. There is so much that needs adjusting and the question was asked as to whether the adjustment could be made while people were awake and going about their business.

The answer was that in time—many, many years time—the adjustment might be made as people raised their consciousness. However, in the long run, did Earth wish to wait more? She is ready now. She no longer wants to wait for people to wake up their consciousness. She has waited for centuries for that to happen. Humanity has been too slow to change. In some instances the dark have gotten darker and in other instances, the Light have become lighter. However, it still is not at the level where the Earth could change in the tremendous way that is needed.

We have often spoken about Earth's needing a new set of clothes. She needs nurturing. Many years ago she was on the verge of giving up and dying out, for the dark had become darker. Therefore, Stasis was brought to the table. Are we going to go ahead with this? Do we have the permission from the Father and the Creator to usurp the free will of humanity? And for this instance we received our answer and yes, we do. In this instance we can. There were many arguments pro and con that were presented to the Creator to see if this could be acceptable.

Therefore, we made a trial run in the public announcements that were recently put out. The messenger has received a great deal of shall we say *flack*, but she was doing her utmost in the way she could receive it as a telepathic receiver. The date for Stasis, however, was not accurate. We wish not to give a date as it can fluctuate so much.

In the next several months this Stasis suggestion will be revisited. We also take into consideration the influence of the different planets and the moon. As you know, the moon has a great influence with your tides and the waters. Since the bodies have a high percentage of water, they are greatly affected by the moon, whether they really realize it or not. All of this has had to be taken into consideration.

Therefore, Stasis has *not* been taken off the table. It is still there, but only as a *possibility* for now. We are watching how humanity is reacting to the different changes of the planet. As you know, the other planets affect each other. Astrologically, you can know how you will be affected also. Mercury is going into retrograde and that planet always plays havoc with communication. Mars in someone's chart plays havoc in whatever house it transverses. There is a purpose you see.

These are guidelines and they are to be respected for what they are. The study of astrology has been around for hundreds and thousands of years. It was a guideline for people. Back in antiquity before computers and the Internet, people needed books of spirituality—their Bibles, the Koran, and the Torah. People also needed the Astrologers. The Goddesses used astrology. Then as with anything else, people distorted the truths about this pure science and gave it dark titles—soothsayers, witches, the devil speaking. Especially, if the Christians are afraid of something, they say it is because of the devil's work, not realizing that much of their fear of the devil was from their own thoughts that they had brought to themselves.

Now, dear friends, I wish to speak more of another subject. We will leave *Stasis* laying on the table in the Council room as a possibility. It has not been shelved. There has come to light the possibility of a planet being fired up and becoming Earth's second sun. Much conjecture of this has also been passed around. Some say Jupiter is a planet and planets can never become a Nova and explode with fire. This is true to a point, but many a planet unknown to science has exploded with too much of its own fire.

Jupiter—the *Jupiter Effect*—is what we are talking about. Jupiter is on the verge of firing, of becoming so hot that she too will blow and glow. People on Jupiter are aware of this and they have been slowly removed to other planets. There are Councils on Jupiter and the Councils are saying *it is time to evacuate*. Therefore, you see that Earth is not the only planet thinking of evacuation.

Now, will this happen? Again it is in the realm of possibility. The planet is running very hot. You know, Readers, planets have destinies also. They have destinies to be born and to die. They have destinies to become a sun if they so choose. We are speaking of Jupiter's destiny. There was a discussion in our Councils whether to pre-fire Jupiter. In other words would it not be more advantageous for those great Beings that carry fire to ignite a planet if that is her destiny and all have been evacuated—to fire that planet while she is in a certain orbit so she will do little harm to other planets that are near her?

It has been argued pro and con whether one ought to fire up Jupiter before she fires and explodes herself. Of course the best time to do it was when she was positioned with Earth's sun being used as a buffer, for Jupiter's firing could explode and that energy would go into Earth's sun, which would cause great sun flares that would bombard the Earth. This would be an event that had never happened before during humanity's consciousness. They would not have been a part of this, so they would not have heard about it.

Again this is on the table. Whether it comes to pass or not in your lifetime is up to you, really. It had been predicted that the Stasis must happen first and then the Jupiter Effect would follow. We say that that is still on the table. We are not the only ones writing about this. It is being passed around on the Internet from several sources.

This Channel first read this on the www.AbundantHope.net site by Candace Frieze. Do not attack the messenger. Is she 100% accurate all of the time? No, but she is a beautiful soul and she is fulfilling her purpose to the best of her ability. Some say she is ego-driven. I say are not all humans in ego at times? Some say she becomes defensive. I say if you were attacked enough would you not become somewhat defensive?

It is very difficult to remain untouched by the criticisms she receives because she is feeling their energies. People do not realize that the words they send to her are full of energy. If the Reader is in disapproval, that is the energy that the author receives. If you are very intuitive and carry a great deal of Light in your body, you will feel this disapproval and feel the judgments many times more than the average person.

Again the messenger, dear friends—do not kill the messenger. If she had never followed her instructions, how would you have heard or known about this? We think it is important for people to know what is *coming down the pike*, so to speak—to know the ideas that are out there. The Masters have scenarios that humanity does not know about until the information is given to it, for it is not in your reality to know this.

Are some people afraid of this Jupiter Effect? Of course they are. People are afraid of things that they do not understand nor know nor have experienced. However, can you put yourself into a position to understand that anything that we from the Spiritual Hierarchy—the Space Brothers of the Spiritual Hierarchy—give to you will be for your highest good, with the least amount of trauma, in the most caring and thoughtful way that we could do it?

You are greatly blessed, our dear ones. You have no idea how much we take you into our hearts and how much we wish for you in every good way that is possible. Do not lose sleep over this Jupiter Effect. It is a possibility and not a probability yet. It is best to stay in the present. Since time is linear on your planet, stay in present time. Do not worry what is in the future. Just know in your heart that you will be in the right place at the right time, even if that is in your bed and you wake up on a ship in another bed that could possibly look just like yours. Or you could wake up and realize that you have had a long nap. Or you could wake up and not realize that three weeks have passed. Once you do realize it, you will realize that you are still up and walking around *healthy, wealthy, and wise,* as the saying goes. Dearest Readers, do not fret so. Be wise. Listen to your souls and bless the messengers who give you the messages. And just because the messages that they are giving you are outrageous to your mind, do not think of them as having turned to the dark. They are *messengers* and they bring messages from the Light.

With that dearest Readers, I will close now. I have spoken about the effects of Stasis and Jupiter. Know that they are still in the realm of possibilities and could happen—maybe not even in your lifetime—but maybe in the lifetime of your children. That is all.

I AM Andromeda Rex.
(10-11-07)

CHAPTER 6- GODDESS QUAN YIN

Well, dearest one, you are ready for another chapter, I see. (Yes, Lord, I am keeping up with you.) So we see, and you are attempting in your mind to figure out how can this book be twenty chapters—of what? I say to you to just keep channeling and you will soon find out. (Yes.) All right, I have confused you enough so I will get down to business—get serious, as Tuella said. We still chuckle over that.

Today will be somewhat less dramatic than what Andromeda has spoken about. I do not think that Stasis and the Jupiter Effect need to be revisited in this book. It may be for others to comment, but keep in mind that those are possibilities and not probabilities yet.

We know that there is fear of the Space Brothers. We have known this for a long time. That again is something that we discuss in our Councils—that is on the table. "How can we alleviate the fear that humanity has of seeing spaceships that look to them like moving tops? What can we do to bring joy, anticipation, excitement; what could we do to help?" Therefore, this chapter is going to be about that—how to bring our presence to humanity without fear.

The speaker whom I am bringing forth has not spoken yet in this book. She is a Goddess and one whom most of you will recognize. I will step aside now and let her speak.

Good morning, dearest Channel and dear, dear Readers, **I AM the Goddess Quan Yin** who watches over so many of you and lovingly receives the devotion that you give to me. Many of the Oriental culture revere me, but I am for all of humanity. Yes, my eyes are somewhat almond shaped, because that is the shape I chose and enjoy. My body is more of the Oriental type. I move in a gentle way—softly, non-intrusively, my long gown swaying. And no, my feet are not bound.

However, I did experience that when I had one of my lifetimes on your planet. I wanted to know what that did to the psyche of the children—the female child. How best to know, but to become one? Therefore, I walked into a body that was already prepared—a body that was a chubby little female, all giggles and smiles. Then her feet were strapped and not allowed to grow.

At first there was little pain. It would be similar to having a tight stocking on your foot. However, I was growing quickly and the bandages started to pinch and my feet started to swell and I cried and cried. Thereby, my mother held me and cooed to me and told me that this was for my betterment. I had not yet grown into the language, so I only cried.

I did not stay in that body that long. I gave that body a merciful death, for I was not interested in the sexual nuances of that day or era. As you have read in your history, little tiny feet of young girls enhanced the men's virility and hence, promiscuity. I was not interested in experiencing that aspect of it. I was only interested in the aspect of what the pain did to the body and hence to the soul.

I was a Goddess when I walked into that body, so I came with consciousness and knew what I was doing and what I had asked for. That was my agreement. *All right I will experience this, but I will end it also when I have gleaned all that I want to know.* I am known as the Goddess of Compassion, Mercy, and Love.

Does not one have to experience pain and suffering in order to be compassionate and to learn to be merciful? Of course you do. As I am coming closer to this Channel, she is feeling the emotions, the energy of compassion. You see it lights up what is left in her body in the memory cells of pain and suffering. She has gone through much in many lifetimes to be the Being that she is now, a Being that is so respected in our spheres.

Now this book speaks somewhat of spaceships and many of you probably do not know that I, Quan Yin, have a spaceship that I have named the *Lotus Blossom.* It is a beautiful ship. Many times I invite Beings of Earth to come visit me on my beautiful ship—to visit me while their body is sleeping. You many not realize it, but the majority of you Readers usually visit the various Goddesses and Masters on their ships. You could even have your own ship if you have reached that level of consciousness.

You see, dear ones, spaceships are very common in our realm. On my ship I cook up succulent Oriental dishes, but I will tell you my little secret. I merely create them through thought. I think of them and remember them and add the spices to them. I smell them and can taste them all by thought as I am creating them, you see. I then program them into a computer box and the box registers every thought that I have given it. I even think of the little Oriental dishes on which the different specialties are presented. I believe that the culinary cooks call it *plating* a particular item. I plate my delectable foods, so that when the people arrive from their sleeping bodies, they have a delicious Oriental banquet awaiting them.

Yeshua had said that we know humanity fears us. I think they would fear even seeing their fairy-godmother appear, as she does in the Cinderella story. Anything they have not seen, anything that they have not perceived as possible, humanity fears. However, some people really would enjoy seeing us Masters, seeing us in our finery, for of course we would dress up for you. Some may be in their space uniforms, but we still would dress keeping you in mind.

There are statuettes of me always in a flowing robe. Since humanity expects me to look like that, that is how I will appear. Of course I will come, for it is my presence that will help calm the audience down. We know there are great expectations for the Christ to appear. He will eventually do his thing on the Mount in Israel. Whether that will be his first landing is still debatable.

Each of us will land in a designated spot. There are Masters who monitor different sectors of the planet. Where to land is an assignment that each of us has. I am not going to tell you where I am going to land. People expect me to land in China. I may. We have had some fun with that, for we say *how would it be for the people in Mexico to see Quan Yin in her spaceship versus the Virgin Mary?* This amuses us to think of the reactions of different people, for the Master who comes may not be the one they reverently hope or expect to come.

We will land all over the planet, you see. Since your planet has the twenty-four-hour time system, it means that a part of your planet is in darkness while another part is in daylight. Therefore, we take that into consideration also. We believe that landing in the daylight would be less stressful for people versus landing in the dark, for so many people correlate darkness with the *booby man*.

Consequently, we attempt to think of the different things that we could do to help humanity not to be afraid. We have a great sense of humor. We love to mix it up a bit and not present ourselves in a stereotypical way in a stereotypical area that is designated only where people think we ought to be. We consider that as being placed in a box. I know that the Mother Mary has often moaned, for Christianity has put her in such a box. She is trying to break that up.

It is hoped that eventually humanity will get used to our presence—get used to the fact that another spaceship has just landed or taken off. At first it will be a great novelty, and in those countries that are always on the verge of some war or other with their tanks, guns, and missiles all pointed and spotless as they parade down the avenues of their cities, those armaments will be pointed at us no doubt. We do not have any intention of letting any of them fire upon us.

You have read or heard, I am sure, that we have the capability of becoming invisible with a certain energy that we can put around us. We can put a certain cover around our ships so that they can look like a cloud in the sky. As Ashtar has said many times, look to the sky, for the cloud that you see moving rapidly across the sky could be one of the ships.

GODDESS QUAN YIN

We would like nothing better than to land and open our doors and have tours come through our ships. We could feed you and entertain you by listening to the angels' music. Oh yes, we will have the angels there also playing their different instruments. They do not only play harps, you understand. They are proficient with many instruments and have beautiful voices. You have heard that term *music from the spheres,* and this is how it will sound. It will lull you into the most peaceful feeling, for it will be pure love entering into your bodies. Would it not be a marvelous party to be moving around meeting the Masters whom you only have read about, eating the exotic foods that we will prepare for you by our Light thoughts, and listening all the while to this music from the spheres? It would be glorious for you, dear Readers, and so enjoyable for us.

You have no idea how much we appreciate the loving energy that you send our way. Whenever anyone thinks of us in love and sends us love and compassion, it fills us and we feel it and are so joyous for you. This is what it would be like if we were able to land and feel your hearts open, feel your awe about the things you are seeing, feel your joy, for it will truly be Heaven on Earth, dear souls. We will bring mercy to those souls that are in pain and mourning their loved ones. We will bring compassion to those who are in grief.

We will bring love to everyone and fill you with the love that we carry. This is our wish. We wish that you will be able to receive it as well and as fully as it has been given to you.

Our technologies are beyond your comprehension, and we have a willingness to share with those who come in peace. Our technologies are not for war. Our technologies are to further the medical field, to further the field of alternative medicine, to further homeopathy, to further the arts and sciences and even those sciences of not only astronomy but astrology. This may surprise many of you, but we believe also that the planets have a great influence on humanity. We do not believe that that is the devil's work. The Creator made the planets, and He is not of the devil (*smile*).

That will be one of the hardest tasks there is, for the Christians on one hand love God and Jesus with all of their heart, but on the other hand carry such fear of the devil and evil. They become so polarized that they cannot change any of their out-moded ideas at all. Thereby, you see we have a daunting task also. Ours is to help you see the Light and yours is to accept the Light when it is offered to you. Our task is to be love and to bring you love, compassion and mercy. Your task is to receive the love, compassion, and mercy when it is given to you.

Consequently, dear friends, we both have our work cut out for us (*chuckles*). However, this we can do, by the love of the Father, this we can do.

With that, my precious souls, I bless you and I am available to any and all who call upon Quan Yin, the Goddess of Mercy, Compassion, and Love.

(*Thank you, Quan Yin, it was so nice to hear from you again.*) You are welcome, dear soul. (*I have a rather mundane query, but there has been a discrepancy as to how to spell your name. Do you spell it with a Q or a K?*) Actually, I do not have a particular preference. It is up to the individual. Q's are fine and K's are fine—whatever you wish, my dear. (*All right, thank you.*) That is all, dear one. (*Thank you, Goddess.*) 10-12-07

CHAPTER 7- COMMANDER ASHTAR

*I am here, dear one; **I AM Yeshua**. (I had just been reading the* Beatitudes *that you had discussed and explained to Glenda Green in her book* Love Without End. *It seems as if whenever I read those, it brings you right in.) Yes, for it puts you deeply into your heart and that is where I meet you always—always in your heart, dearest one.*

If humanity would love and live in its heart, how much more joyous Earth would be. We would not be having to write this book, for we would have landed and walked among you and you would have greeted us with joy, love, and fellowship.

We do not seek a reverence from you, for you see that usually stems from a religious training. Now there is a correct way for students to have devotion, respect, and if you wish to use that word reverence *for their Master teachers. If it is correct and not possessive and not in awe, there is nothing wrong in knowing your teachers' highest achievements. Not everyone is at the same level of consciousness. Every soul is growing and we love all of you, each and every one of you.*

Therefore, when we land, let it be with joy and yes, even anticipation, for we come with much love in our hearts. It is so gratifying when we are loved back! You know that, Readers, in your own relationships, how many of you out there are married and yet your lover does not fully give back to you with a deep love, so that when you hug you really feel him or her deeply in your heart?

You can be married for years and yet know that something is missing. What is missing, you see, is that your partner is not capable of deeply loving. He or she may have what we term a shallow heart. *It has no depth to it. The person could be kind and giving to you, but not capable of full love, for you see that stems from the parenting that he/she had received. If there was not the full depth of love from the parents, then the child would not grow up with that—would not know that. That is something then that that person will learn.*

That is what makes it so wonderful when people are finally, shall we say, hooked up with their Twin Flame, for the love there , you see, is immeasurable. It is total giving. Consequently, when we come together, we flames, each to the other it is the most gratifying and endearing, loving, experience one can ever know. Each of you will experience this at some time in your growth.

Each of you has a Twin Flame and each of you will find that person one of these days. Most of the flames are separated, doing his/her progression, waiting until they can finally join. Some of you when you come aboard our ships, your flame will be there. This Channel's flame is on her ship, waiting. It is a glorious moment when the flames meet.

Now I have gotten a little off track there, as we are starting a new chapter, so it is time to bring in the next Presenter. I think I will let this be a surprise, which always causes a bit of unrest with this Channel, for she does like to know beforehand. I will come back afterwards. (Thank you, Yeshua.)

Hello once again to our Readers and to this Channel. **I AM Ashtar.** *(Ashtar, hello; I might have* *known, chuckles.)* Yes, it was quite an evening last night with Victoria (*Liljenquist)* and her presentation, looking at the different space ships that she had photographed. As you can surmise, we were there and in great numbers. It amused us when you all went outside and stared at the sky, hoping to see the ships with your naked eyes. Not everyone can see us nor did we show ourselves last night.

However, back to another subject. I wish to bring up some information that we could say is grave news. The planet is not vibrating at the rate that we wished she could. She is slipping again somewhat. It is not that because she is not willing, but it is Humanity's thought-forms, Humanity's greed, Humanity's willingness to war against each other. Of course we are aware that there are many that do not wish war.

In America the government proclaims that things are getting better, that the war is lessening and they will be bringing troops home in a few years. As the more conscious people know, that is all white-wash. Or I can say, using my favorite phrase, *horse-putty.* That is horse-putty. The people of America know that that war is going nowhere fast in Iraq.

Afghanistan is flaring up again. It reminds me of a volcano. It quiets down and then it comes up again. It erupts again because of the greed and the polarity in those countries. As many of you know, Afghanistan's economy is more or less built on the poppy trade. Those poor, poverty stricken families get a taste of a little money from selling a poppy crop that can be turned into heroin and then when there is an attempt by the government to eradicate the fields, they are without money and means to support their many children. It is out of balance.

That is what is happening to the whole world; it is out of balance. It has become a grave situation. What makes it such a miserable choice is that many must die in order to bring balance. Those countries that used to be beautifully populated and irrigated so that there was green vegetation have become an eyesore. The pictures shown on television look to be as if there is hardly any water. People are in their dusty robes and turbans reeking from lack of bathing, scratching out a living. That term the *rich become richer and the poor become poorer* is certainly true in those countries.

The Overlords of the poppy fields have their riches like Sultans of the past. The poor farmers have little to show for their efforts. If you put it in the terms of dollars and cents, the Overlords are getting approximately 95 cents to the dollar and the farmer is getting 5 cents. Those are such inappropriate wages, even if they are wages of sin. At least let there be some balance to it. But there is none. It is similar to throwing a bone to a starving animal.

Readers, you wonder why Mother Earth is in pain. You only have to look at those two countries, Afghanistan and Iraq, to know how that grieves her. And we haven't even mentioned the Overlords in South America, or the people of Sudan that are murdered daily.

There is only greed and evil, so the Earth slips. She is trying desperately to hang on—to claw her way up to the fifth dimension. The fourth dimension is a transition period and it takes a long while to come to the fifth dimension, for you must change—the energy must change. There must be joy and love and giving of one's self.

We speak of other people making transitions to other dimensions. A planet is no different. In fact her burdens are much greater, for she has the burden of all of humanity. Whereas you, Reader, are singular. Take the griefs that you have experienced in your lifetime and multiply that by millions and millions of what the planet has suffered.

I AM Ashtar and I bring you this message, this Sunday morning of October 14, 2007. When will the change occur? When can I greet you with more joy, for it is up to you, humanity. We have talked about the Stasis and how to bring balance to the planet. It is the strife in the world that I have just talked about—the greed, the unkind thoughts, the lack of love and caring—that is why Stasis is still on the Council table. It is a strong possibility and getting stronger each day.

In fact since this book has a way to go before it is finished and then there are always a few more months in the publishing process, the Earth may already have gone through its Stasis. It would be a time that we could land and help bring balance. We could clean the pollution, clean the air.

Victoria Liljenquist was saying last night (*in a presentation she gave at the Arizona Enlightenment Center*) that she was having trouble breathing in Arizona because of the pollution and the dust in the air—the quality of the air. There are states all over America where the air is not pure. It has long been known in the Los Angeles area— the pollutants, called *smog*. It has long been known that smog has invaded Arizona. One could say that every major city in America has bad air—has smog.

People migrate to Colorado for the higher elevations. However, Denver has its bad air also. One must get up into the mountains and then they have the problem of the severe weather in the winters, which will be getting more severe. There is not one state in America where one could breathe pure air. Hawaii is somewhat different in that it has its trade winds that blow and circulate the air. However, from our advantage point we can see a ring that goes around the larger islands and that air is not pure. Honolulu has grown so rapidly and is so over-crowded that the air is no longer pure. The firing of the cane fields on the outskirts adds to the bad air. The trade winds blow it clean and then the fires continue.

Therefore, Readers, no matter where you are those of you in Iowa who read these books, those of you in Georgia, Virginia, and Pennsylvania have your problems also with the pollutants . People do not realize that you cannot keep running your gas-filled automobiles, adding to the pollutants. The manufactures say that they will have clean gas-fueled cars, clean energy, but it is always years away—2018 or whatever number they come up with which is not in reality. It is not realism. And yet it is not feasible to stop right now, this minute, for it takes years of retooling to make these automobiles clean.

Consequently, dear Readers, you see why we keep speaking about Stasis even though Yeshua was thinking that we more or less had been done with it in this book. It was my listening to Victoria last evening at the Arizona Enlightenment Center that our precious Heather Clarke and her friends created, listening to Victoria and hearing her say that she had been guided to leave, for the air quality had gotten worse in the last few months. She also has reasons for moving to Colorado for she has karma there. But she felt that the pollutants had increased over the last few months in Arizona.

She is correct in that because Arizona has not had a sufficient amount of rain to wash it away. It has no trade winds. The wind that it receives many times has copious amounts of dust in it, so that everything is covered in dust as it makes its way across the State. It seeps under the window sills. There is so much building going on so that the contractors are fined if they do not make any attempt to keep the dust down as their huge machinery rakes up the desert. All of this we see, dear friends, from the ships. Our instruments give us this reading and the negativity is reaching ever higher, also. Our instruments show this. Crime is on the rise.

There has always been a high crime in stealing of automobiles simply because people from across the border have found this a lucrative way of making money. They are experts in breaking into your car and driving it south of the border where it can be sold for high prices; or they can dismantle it and take just what they want—the new tires, or some other apparatus on the car. All of this can be sold. These cars are money makers. I am speaking of Arizona, for this is where this Channel lives, but New Mexico also has the problem, as does Texas and California.

The earthquakes are coming, dear friends. The water tsunamis are coming. Who of you are prepared? We are coming, dear friends. Who of you are prepared (*smile*)? The time has come to get real, as the saying goes. It is not fantasy any longer. It is real. The danger is real. Those people who are less aware go about their business and have no idea what is about to happen.

Those people who spend their time in the movie houses watching the cops and robbers come up with more sophisticated ways to rob or kill someone that is what fills their minds as they leave the theater. Others are busy playing the video games—which usually depict the good versus the bad killing people. Why does it always have to involve killing?

There seems to be categories here. You have the cops and robbers. You have the New Age type of stuff—la-la land. You have the religions, which is one religion trying to convert the other. When Christianity decided it must bring the Jews into its religion and that Christianity was the only way to go, they do not know what they are talking about. It would bring Christian Fundamentalists great joy if they brought a Buddhist into their camp. People always think their religion is the one. Yet if people could just leave the whole concept that there needs to be a religion, they could think in terms of Spirituality. Let there be Spirituality. The majority of the people on this planet need to learn what true Spirituality is.

Spirituality is very simple, for it is love. *Love your neighbor as you would love yourself* is what the Lord said, but you see if you have a greedy person, a miserly person, a person who cannot love then he or she would treat the neighbor the same way and not think very much of that neighbor. Love is what makes the world go round and it is not happening. The Earth Mother is not happy. She is weeping, crying out for help and we, the Spiritual Hierarchy and the Spiritual Space Brothers in the Galactic Command have been given permission by God the Father and the Creator to help this Earth.

We have sat many an hour at the Council table presenting different ideas, stating the different objections to them, or stating the different ways that they could be acceptable—the pros and cons. We have many suggestions on the table and have shelved very few of them. One of the suggestions that we did shelve was to evacuate every single person off the planet and let the planet do her thing. Let the volcanoes blow; let the earthquakes quake; let the waters roar forth in the tsunamis; let it cleanse the planet. Then start again to re-seed it with the higher consciousness Star Seeds, the Lightweavers and bring them down once again into clean, healthy, loving bodies. However, we shelved that one. We saw with the capability that we had 30-40 years ago that we could not do it in the way that we wished. Mass evacuation was not feasible. We shelved that.

However, parts of it were still discussed and we talked about it and we decided that perhaps by giving humanity its free will, it would give them a choice and let them decide whether they wanted to experience all the coming Earth changes, or did they wish to be lifted up and out. Those are choices. And those are on the table and those are what we are deciding to implement.

Those are no longer possibilities, dear friends. They are probabilities. It is probable that we will lift some of you off **if** you so choose. We will lift you up to us where there is clean, pure air, abundant food that is beautifully prepared, delicious and good for you, where there are clean clothes, bathing facilities and comfortable rooms. You can even play by the beautiful shores or hike in the mountains. We have all of that on the Mother ships. You have no idea.

The Mother ships are like another world. They are like a Utopia. You do not just sit and do nothing, for everyone needs to grow. You are given choices where you can be of service. You are given choices as to what you would wish to learn. You are given choices up there and of course we will give you a time to reflect. We will give you as much time as you wish, but we will not let you become bored or restless.

Our ships are capable of moving, flying if you want to say, but even we use common sense. We do not land when a planet such as Earth is having her volcanoes spew and the earthquakes rumbling in her cleansing. It would be foolhardy. We are not about to land in an area that we know will be covered in water. Therefore, you see we are cautious also and we make every attempt to make it safe for all concerned, for we must think of the safety of our ship and the safety of our crew. As I have said, we are not foolhardy. We will make every attempt to help people escape some catastrophe that is happening in a particular place if it does not endanger our ship. We would then use teleportation. We would send the beam down and beam that person up, if we can ascertain that the person's vibratory rate is high enough to withstand the energy-beam.

We are determined, dear Readers, we are determined to help Mother Earth. Since you are all living on her, we are determined to help you in any way that we possibly can. However, it is basically up to you. It is up to you to raise your consciousness. It is up to you to be in your heart, to broaden your Light, to embrace your fellow men and women. It is up to you! We offer you the choices; we offer you the choices. It is then up to you to pick and choose and to receive.

Those of you who can receive will have the easier time. Those of you who cannot receive—in your own lifetime people give to you and you cannot receive—you will have a more difficult time, because we are offering you a choice to experience a beautiful way of living on our ships for a while. It is not to be for eternity. We would not be able to have you for an eternity (*chuckles*). It would be for a duration that can only be measured by what is going on on Earth.

Receive us, dear friends, for we come with love. We do not judge you. It is not judging you, but discernment. If a child is walking along the street in the gutter during the rain, for it is playing in the water flowing down the street, do we judge that child—the bad child? No, we merely discern that that child is going to have wet shoes. It is not judging. This Channel when she was a little girl would put on her rain-coat and her rain-boots and walk to school. However, she walked in the gutters where the water, leaves, sticks, and the mud were. She sloshed her way to school, enjoying every moment. However, when she took her boots off in the school cloak-room, she discovered that her shoes had gotten wet at the same time. Consequently, she learned a lesson, you see. Did we judge her? Of course not, for she was a child playing and this gave her pleasure.

Therefore, we do not judge you, dear friends, but discern what you are doing and we can feel the joy or the sorrow that it will bring. Thereby, dear friends, choose wisely. We are offering many choices. Choose wisely. That is all that I wish to say this morning.

I AM Ashtar of the Galactic Federation of Light and I am a member of the Spiritual Hierarchy and my Commander-in-Chief is your Lord Sananda Kumara whom I also call Brother and my dearest friend and companion.

(Thank you, Ashtar, that was a potent chapter!)
Yes, dear one, we are greatly concerned. Ashtar, over and out.

All right, dear one, that was my friend! He is concerned, for the energy has taken a dive, shall we say. So he is concerned. I believe that this will do it for today. Please stay in your Light and consciousness. Stay in peace, for it is greatly needed.

CHAPTER 8- LORD SUREA, SIRIUS

Good morning everyone, I AM Yeshua, sitting a little early today. As I was telling this Channel, any time is a good time. Any time that you can sit and think of love, compassion, peace in the world, the various Spiritual Masters, the Space Brothers, and keeping your thoughts on the Christ Consciousness, that is a good time—the appropriate time.

We have not spoken since last Sunday, October 14, when Ashtar was telling you that the Earth had taken a little dip. You see, on your path to consciousness, evolution, climbing up the ladder, it is never a steady climb upwards. It is two paces up and one back, three paces up and two back. This seems to be a time when your blessed Earth has taken several steps back. However, she will get back on track, for you see it is humanity that will change its ways that will make it possible for her to keep evolving.

Some people forget that she is an actual living Being—a powerful one at that. Put yourself in her shoes as if this whole huge planet was simply you! You would not need the people on your back to raise your consciousness. You would just keep growing. That is what she is doing. She will shake off the laggards, the ones who are taking up space and doing nothing—what Ashtar calls "Cosmic Feng Shui"—taking up space without accomplishing anything. They are blocking the energies from flowing. She will shake those souls off her back with the coming earthquakes.

Now it seems as if we are forever talking about the dark side. It so happens that it is that time in history. When it is so prevalent, it does take center stage. However, lest you forget, there are of course pockets of consciousness where people carry the Christ Consciousness and are hard workers in their fields. You will find them in fields of the helping careers. People in the helping professions are usually of the Light.

Now that does not mean by any means that they are all in the fifth dimension, nor that they are working for pure love of service. There are those who are working to make the mighty dollar. However, most of the people in the helping professions are in touch with their souls and are urged on by their souls. Yet, many are still in the fourth dimension rather than the fifth.

Now this morning there will be a new Presenter and it is a male figure of magnificence on his own planet. So without further words from me, I will let him step forward and then I will come back if it is necessary. (All right, thank you.)

Good morning, Readers and to this Channel, it is good to be back once again. I have spoken to you before in Book FIVE (*Messages from the Heavenly Hosts*), and **I AM** known as **Lord Surea**. I come from Sirius. It might sound as if we are always "serious." But since it is a planet, it will have its humor as well as its serious side. I hope this morning to give you a little bit of both.

Some of you may know that I come many times through our Emissary, Sheldan Nidle, for he has been with us several times during his lifetime on our ships. He is from Sirius himself.

Yeshua was telling me and we have noticed that the planet has stumbled backward somewhat. But we like to bring hope to people and to let you know that whenever she stumbles, we are there to help balance her again, to pick her up and gently set her on her path again.

You have been told in the past that many times when the dark is getting ready to leave, they will fight harder since they know the game is up. They become more aggressive. They become less cautious, and hence their acts can become more serious. But never fear, because they will not be allowed to use nuclear power. Most of them know this by now and know it is a lost cause so why bother? Sometimes they do it just for the pure pleasure of seeing if they *could* drop a nuclear device, but then realize that they are no longer able to. We are able to control that aspect very clearly and very strongly.

Many of you have read that there could possibly be another 9/11 happening all over again. There will be some of you Readers who are not aware that 9/11 was not a terrorists' attack per se. It was set up by your government. Any terrorists who played a part in it were given handsome rewards.

As more and more citizens of America learn about this, and if the information is repeated enough, some of the truth must seep in to those die-hards who refuse to hear or believe truth. You will find this in your military, your departments of defense, your police force, your firemen, many senior citizens and the strong politicians. They cannot let go of their erroneous beliefs and believe that your presidency was stolen. It was not a true democratic election by any means.

Even your members of the Supreme Court played into that and did not truthfully vote the way their soul had guided them. It was a set up, a distortion of the facts. The votes were stolen. Look at all the controversy that you had over the "hanging chads" and the fraudulent voting machines, many of which have not been fixed yet. There was so much controversy around the voting part of it that the truth never could get in. Al Gore was cheated out of the position to which he had been elected.

However, look at how he has risen above all of that. He did not let that break him. He has continued on the path, being of service and bringing attention to the public of the changes that need to be made for the environment. Now will he become president this time? Only if he enters the ring. His opponent would be Hillary Clinton who is a fighter. If he does not enter the ring, she could very well become the first woman president.

There are no strong candidates on the Republican side. One, Rudy Giuliani, is a strong possibility, but only because he was at one time mayor of New York City. His skirts are not clean, nor are most politicians of New York City wearing clean skirts. Crime is prevalent in that large city. If you are a Republican, people, the pickings are slim, for no Republican will win.

Barack Obama has a better chance of being vice president than he does of being president, which is all right since he is young. Dennis Kucinich's value is not well known enough for him to be president, but he also would make an excellent vice president. The ticket of Gore and Kucinich would win. Whether the public will agree with me, we will wait and see.

There has been much talk about impeachment, to impeach the president or to impeach the vice president. We do not see this as happening, for the dark forces still have control, and they would keep jamming the proposals so that the votes are never there. Congress has done little work these last four years. The politicians are so centered on their own game plans that they do little work. Many or almost the majority of Congress are fourth dimensional people. Very few have made it into the fifth dimension as yet, a dimension of love, of doing for the good and being of WE the people.

As you look at your present Congress, the members are struggling. Their egos are large and there are some who are still in third dimensional thinking and using the lower centers—power and sex. Those having the sex scandals are pretty much third dimensional or are just starting the fourth dimension. Their consciousness has not risen. For men it is called *being below the belt*.

Now why have I gotten off onto the political scene? Because I have been talking about the dark energies. The political scene in Washington for all of its rhetoric is pretty much of the dark. They have done little to further the comfort of America. Health care has not been reformed. The pharmaceutical companies are still in control. The lobbyists are winning. The little guy, the homeless are not being taken care of.

This Channel was watching a bit of television showing the homeless people and one young man was walking barefooted everyplace because he had no shoes nor socks. In the land of plenty, that is a sad sight to see.

America is polarized as you know — the haves and the have-nots. The middle class is disappearing.

The farmers cannot scratch out a living, so they sell their land to the large developers who come in and build huge developments. The farmers no longer take pleasure in their crops, for there is little return for the long hours that they put into farming. They get up at dawn to care for their animals, start the plowing or irrigation and go to bed at sundown. With little rest in between and with little relaxation, many find that the only way to bring any joy to their life is with alcohol, which is never a good solution. Their wives also are exhausted, cooking and canning and trying to make ends meet. The rich get richer and the poor get poorer. The government's subsidizing the farmers is only giving them an incentive to not work.

There needs to be a new administration. There needs to be new energy. However, the new administration will have to have survival skills also. It will have to have strong leadership, for there will be so much going on with the climate, the oceans, with the land-tremors and devastating earthquakes. This time will be a major trial for anyone coming into the presidency.

Al Gore has the experience as the former vice president and thereby could handle most of what comes up for him. He also would be open to having the ships land. He would be open to telling the military to stand down and to lower their weapons. This is the kind of administration that you will need.

Now what can I say that will bring hope to you, dear Readers? The hope comes from your Space Brothers. The hope comes from the technology that we can give to you.

The hope comes from the medical ships that we have, for we can teach your healers how to heal the bodies.

I would say that one of the major hurdles for humanity will be to get over its fear, for you cannot receive anything, help or otherwise, when you are cowering with fear or striking out with fear. There will always be those people who will have hidden guns and will shoot first and talk later. Those are the ones whom we would need to neutralize in some way. Our love will be poured out on humanity, but for those who cannot receive it, they would not be willing to accept new ideas.

Today is a beautiful morning in Arizona. This Channel lives near Luke Air Force Base and the planes frequently fly over her house, practicing their landings or whatever their lesson is for the day. This Channel's former husband was a Navy flier, and many times he would be out on assignment practicing night landings and instruments— always practicing. Therefore, she does not mind the jets flying over her house, for she knows these young men and women are learning their trade—honing their expertise, doing the souls' purpose. She prays for them, sending prayers of safety, for as they become older not all of them will live to tell their children about their adventures.

I wish you good day, dear Readers, and may the Lord on High bless all of you and keep you safe. We are here; we are ready and we await only the sign from on High that we may come to you. That day is almost here.
I AM Lord Surea.

All right, dear one, back once again. (My gosh that was a political chapter. I am wondering whether to censor any of it, to leave the names out, etcetera.) No, dear one, do not censor. He has his reasons and one of them is that it is time for humanity to know what goes on behind the scenes. It is taking their rose-colored glasses off and letting them see reality. Bit by bit there will be more people who will be willing to accept the fact that your president and your government and media lie to you most the time. Accept it for what it is; see it for what it is. You can always call upon the Father to bless them, to bring Light to them and let it go. Blessed are they who seek the Kingdom of Heaven. I AM Yeshua.

(Author's note: I wrote the following for Book FIVE and will repeat it here. Sheldan Nidle wrote an extraordinary book entitled Your First Contact, *published in 2000. He goes into great detail about his meeting with the Sirians. He writes, "Lord Surea is an Aspect of Mother/Father God in charge of sacred Lineage and Councils of Heaven who carry out the divine plan." Sheldan's book is packed with diagrams of star systems and their ships. I know no other book of this caliber. I highly recommend it. He and his partner, Colleen, have recently moved from Hawaii to San Mateo, California. To order his book, go to* www.paoweb.com. *)*

CHAPTER 9- CHRIST MICHAEL

Good morning once again, Readers, and to this Channel. We are back together once again—I, to give you a new chapter and for you to read it. Each chapter is a surprise for this Channel, as I hope it will be for all of you.

Therefore, I will get serious here (chuckles) and get down to business. Although He needs no introduction, it is my greatest privilege to introduce our Father who wears many hats and is called by many names. The name He has chosen to be called today is Christ Michael. Without further words from me, I am honored to have Him speak in our book.

Good morning to all, **I AM Christ Michael**. I am delighted once again to speak from this Channel's perspective. I have come for each one of her books and given a message. I have worn many hats—some of which you would term as your *religious hats* coming as the Father or as God. The name I prefer to be known by this morning is *Christ Michael*. I am the Creator of your world. I am the Creator of this Universe, Nebadon.

There has been much reported of late as to when the ships will land. Some call it First Contact, others just say, spaceships. All are correct. There has been talk of Stasis, the Big Sleep, and of the Jupiter Effect. Again both are correct. Many of you are confused by the different propositions that we have laid out on the Council table.

However, we have given the information to our Messengers to bring forth by way of the Internet so that the world will know of our ideas of what is going on. We have studied long and hard as to what is best for all concerned. I

93

am able to project different Aspects of Myself, so that I am very much present at these conferences—these great Councils. There are many of the grand Masters present, the grand Archangels, the Spiritual Hierarchy of the highest level. We sit and discuss what is a possibility for this beloved Earth.

What could be a possibility to help Earth remove her dark web that others have woven around her? The dark Cabal is in its last throes. It is like a spoiled child, one who has controlled, one who is selfish and does not want to bow down to the wishes of its parents. It stomps its feet in tantrums and shouts obscenities. If that does not work, it weeps copious tears—manipulates—anything to keep from having to obey.

These naughty children of the dark are being showered with Light, given choices—tough love—for they are My children. As you parents know, we must be strict and practice that tough love. These children of Mine who have refused to come out of the shadow, refused to acknowledge that they have a heart, will be removed to another planet that is just for them.

They will be among their peers. They will not be allowed to bother anyone else again. They will come to their senses, shall we say, after many millions of years. You have heard of the living hell where there is a void, where there is nothing that grows. There is nothing that is propagated. There is no beauty; there is no song. There is very little sun. There is light, but in shadow. It is a void place—what some of the religious people would say is truly hell.

However, they will be among their peers! They will be able to rejoice in the way that they see fit, for they will soon all look alike. Therefore, those dark ones, you see, will be removed never to return to this planet. I will not visit them. I will have angels that watch from above. But there are no visitation rights on that planet.

Meanwhile on my beloved Earth, my beautiful Gaia will be going to the Light ever more strongly, reaching for the higher levels of consciousness. She will no longer be thought of as the schoolhouse for the recalcitrant pupils—a planet on the other side of the tracks, shall we say. Actually, she will be sought out for her beauty, her wildlife, and vegetation that is beyond description on many other planets. She will be My planet, the planet I hold dear to My Heart.

We have talked about Stasis before, or you can look it up on the Internet and read about it (www.AbundantHope.net). I look forward to Stasis. I look forward to humanity's being in the deep sleep where I can walk among My sleeping children, kiss the little babies. When they awake, they will not remember that they have been kissed by Me, by God.

You see what my kiss will do—it is the kiss of the Holy Spirit—it will bring them consciousness; it will bring them all the gifts. They will have the second sight. They will have the ability to heal others as well as themselves. They will have all the gifts that astound people to this day. People think of the different gifts as being psychic—a term that they have used. However, for Me it means being more conscious and the person will have risen in consciousness, touched by the hand of God.

In the next days and months, there will be many changes occurring. There will be many political changes, for the Light that is coming onto the planet will seep into everyone's *attic*. The Light is shining upon anyone who is harboring lies, distortions, greed, embezzlement, any of those darker games. Nothing can stay hidden. All will seep forward and those of you in the darker sexual games all will be lit up. You will see people turning themselves in or getting caught on purpose or confessing.

Many of your priests will come forward. Everything of the dark will be unveiled. It will not all happen over night, for it does take time. But you will see an increase in what we call the *Confessional*. There will be an increase of confessions to the media, for people do not want to carry that burden around any longer. Therefore, there will be an increase of people who had harbored the dark who now come to the Light.

There will be an increase in weather changes. Places that rarely have tornadoes will have tornadoes. States that were considered wet states are now dry states. Georgia in America is having especially a difficult time with drought. The Plains in America have experienced extreme flooding. Now, America, you are coming into your winter months. You will have snow storms that will set new records.

Those of you in the Gulf states, and I am including Arizona in that because this Channel lives there, will find there will be more seasonal changes going on. Arizona will experience a colder winter than it has had. When its rainy season comes, it will rain copious amounts. The lakes will fill once again.

As California goes through its changes, the oceans will creep into the shorelines more and more until a great portion will be under water. That is all part of the cleansing and the changes in the weather, for the weather patterns will change.

More and more people are getting skin rashes and Shingles, Eczema, Psoriasis, and what this Channel calls *blood freckles,* where it looks as if someone has splattered you with tiny red freckles on particular places—the tops of your legs from the thighs on down, or one arm and across the neck. Some experience extreme pain as it goes into the nerve endings. All of this is associated with the energies coming onto the planet—the strongest energies yet. And they will be even more so.

It is very difficult at this time to keep your body in balance. Bodies must stay balanced. You need to exercise where you can. For those older people whose joints do not allow that fully, march in place whenever you think of it. Bend when you can; swing your arms when you can; breathe deeply. The secret is to keep moving, even when it is difficult to get in and out of chairs. Raise yourself up and out at least once an hour. Keep moving.

The energy is difficult on everyone. You younger people need to practice your compassion, for you will find that many of your grandparents are having a difficult time with their joints. It is the energy and that is a hard concept for people to realize. If you can, think of being in a sphere and someone is pouring this water on it so hard that it practically dents the sphere—think of it as the energy being liquid, although it is not. It builds a pressure and it is the pressure that is bombarding the bodies.

Many bodies will be making their transitions, coming back to Nirvana and Me. However, I am in their hearts and they can always reach Me there. I am for everyone on the Earth. People condemn Me for the killings, but that is all men's/women's choices—the free will that the Creator has given you and We follow His wishes. I do not step in and make your diseases. I do not step in and create the disasters for your deaths. That is all of your choosing—the choices that you have made centuries ago, coming back to haunt you.

97

America, when you elect governments where the leaders are not pure and lead you into wars, know that all of this will be changing. Do not expect drastic changes overnight once the election happens, however. It always takes a while for a president to settle in. Whenever there is a change in an administration, it always takes a while—the adjustment period. And we will watch to see what America does.

The voting machines are not accurate so we will watch. I cannot interfere, nor will I. It will be what it will be. As Sananda once said, *what was was and what is is.* That is the way the election will be. In the new administration, what was was and what is is.

My dear friends and Readers, it is My dream for you and yes, God can have a dream, it is My dream for you that those of you of the Light will reach ever higher and fill your bodies so full of Light that you are like a star-burst. It is My dream that those of you who are still walking in the shadow will go to the Light before you will have to be lifted off to the void-planet.

You know it is such a simple thing. Merely let go and move into your heart. Some of you are so embedded in the dark that you become puppets, following what anyone has told you to do, getting your body parts pierced, your tongue pierced—any place that you can stick a ring you do it and cringe with pain as it happens. Why are you mutilating your body so? As Sananda once said the only sin that he sees when there is no sin is hurting the body.

The body is a sacred vehicle for you. It is a gift for you. Why do you mistreat it? Do you mistreat your pet animals that way? And yes, the animal shelters will show you that you do. You know there is a difference between dyeing your hair different colors and having different hair cuts versus piercing your body in order to hang rings on it and covering your body with tattoos. That was an ancient practice, primitive and three dimensional. Rise higher; raise your consciousness and do not injure your body so.

Smokers, those of you who are into drugs and alcohol—the addictions—know that those are all sins against the body, if you wish to use that term. Yes, some bodies are more beautiful than others, for it is in their genetic line. But those bodies have been created and molded through your thought forms. To take beautiful bodies and feed them alcohol until they are addicted, to feed them, to binge them with foods and fats until they weigh 300 pounds or more, those are sins against the body. They are harmful.

Hollywood is rampant with beautiful bodies, not only women, but men—handsome men that are addicted, addicted to the alcohol and cocaine and to yes, even sex. Why do you treat your body so? Why cannot you love it? The only thing We can say is that you probably do not realize that your body is a gift.

Little girls are given precious dolls as gifts and they love their dolls, for they are seeing themselves in doll form. They are practicing being mothers. There is so much beauty that is given to the children and then so much that is harmful. Raise your consciousness. Come towards Me and not in a religious sense. Come to Me in a pure Spiritual sense.

I took the opportunity to walk your Earth. I walked it with Sananda-Esu-Immanuel. That was a time in your biblical history. You know, not too many people will accept the point that I, God the Father, was in that Body! That was not My son; that was Me, My manifestation. It was My Body and they wanted to crucify a man and did not realize that they would be crucifying God, the Father! When you put it into that context, it is shocking, is it not?

You see people have separated Me so much from themselves that when I actually created a Body so that I could walk in it and know what it was like to walk in the world that I had created, people would try to kill Me. I now knew what it was like. Did they succeed? Of course not. I left; I left the country and went to the land of the Avatars where there are many Gods and they are appreciated, revered and loved. They can take any form that they wish, as is shown with the Hindu God Ganesh who has the Elephant trunk that he has chosen to keep. We were all Gods together there.

I found that life was not a bed of roses, for the dark hearts and thoughts of people were always surrounding Me. I left that body to go back to the Earth and then I arose. Many people who read this will not quite understand it, but that is all right also. They will not be able to believe that I, Christ Michael, actually created a human body that I entered. It was My Body. It was My Life. I was known throughout your world as Yeshua ben Joseph. I will not go into all the biblical nuances where the Christians have distorted it with their way of thinking nor would the Jews understand. But it was My Body.

I now am aboard your ships. Sometimes I am in My Light Body or I am just pure Energy. That is why you feel so much love when you enter the ships, for it is My Energy.

I believe I have said all that I needed to have said. The days ahead, dear Readers, the months ahead will be difficult for so many of you. And yet those of consciousness will continue to be of service. They will continue sending their messages out on the Internet. They will write the books. They will stand by as Emissaries.

Readers, there may be Stasis. There may be the Jupiter Effect. There will be First Contact in our landings but much remains subject to timing. We have been discussing this for a few years. We now think the time is now. But our *now* is somewhat different from your *now*, so this is the time where you will have to sit it out and be surprised. That is as factual as I can make it.

I will now leave you, dear Readers. I Am Christ Michael, your Father, your God, the God of your planet and Universe.

All right, dear one, shall we call it a day? (Yes, who could follow God?) That is true. You experienced another Aspect of Him did you not? (Yes.) Just type it up and do not question it. It is so. And move, move your body. (Yes, thank you, Lord.) You are welcome. We will be back in a couple of days. (10-20-07, 10:15 AM)

Your Space Brothers and Sisters Greet You

CHAPTER 10- ARCHANGEL MICHAEL

Good morning everyone, I AM Yeshua, still here and you are still writing and we're bringing forth another chapter. This will be the tenth chapter, so you see we are approximately half finished. We could make this book shorter, but there are still some things that we want to bring to your attention. There are still Presenters on assignment, shall we say, for we did speak with all of them.

We set agreements, for when we plan a book, we do not just start out; we call forth people whom we would like to say a few words. We do not dictate to them as to what they must talk about. We do not set parameters—you can only talk about this but not that. We leave it entirely up to them. However, we do give them the flavor of the book. In other words, we say we wish to be writing a book on the Space Brothers. Would you like to be a Presenter? I have not had one say NO yet, which is gratifying I must admit, for they too have their free will (chuckles). Now that was a little bit of humor, I hope you can tell, but it pretty much works like that.

All right, take some deep breaths, Channel, and be in that heart of yours and your Causal body. The next person to come forth does not need an introduction, for he always has a chapter in our books and a place in our hearts. I will step back and let him come forward and introduce himself. I will come back when he is finished. (All right, Lord, thank you.)

Good morning everybody, it is nice to be back once again; or I can say it is nice to be called back, for we greatly enjoy putting in our two cents worth in each of this Channel's books. Some wonder why one would have

Archangels on board ships, so I had better tell you right up front that **I AM Archangel Michael** coming once again to speak.

Your Archangels are very much a part of this Space Command. Why would we not be? We help the Father. Wherever He goest, we go! You see, we have a different outlook than others do. We come from the Angelic realm, and many times our point of view is slightly different from the point of view of other Beings and Masters who have laid their cards on the table. It does not mean we tell them what to do. It just means we add another flavor, another perspective so that a particular proposition would carry various ideas and would address various issues.

The issues that Archangels address while aboard ship preparing to land would be regarding the safety of all concerned. It is important to have safety of the ship and its occupants as well as the safety of the people who may surround us. This is where we with our areas of expertise can use our energies to impress upon people not to be afraid and that we come with love.

Humanity has heard of the Archangels and has heard of me, Archangel Michael, throughout millions of years. And yet if I were to step out of the spaceship onto the deck that we will have projected out, people would not recognize me. I would have to wear my costume and carry my sword, blazing with blue energy. They would be disappointed if I did not wear wings. However, we do not use them. I could make some, but they would be for decorative purposes only (*chuckles*). We will dress so people will know who we are, but we will not be coming with wings. Now will this disappoint people? Probably, but it puts them into a different reality.

ARCHANGEL MICHAEL

It is time that people address their realities, for we are speaking of Spirituality versus religiosity. The religions have us with wings. They have us appearing as men, but we have our counterparts (*Faith is Michael's*) who are female; so a woman Archangel could also be appearing without wings.

Many eons ago I came to your planet. I wanted to know what it would be like to touch ground; what it would be like to reach out and touch a human; what it would be like to actually hear a human speak. Now of course I have come through many channels, some more specifically than others—those that I over light. But it is different from when you are actually walking the Earth and you are watching how a human reacts.

I would go out to the countryside and, since I am able to appear whenever and wherever I wish, I just chose to be there. I do have to lower my energy somewhat and although it is somewhat uncomfortable, I do not tarry there for long, but just long enough to be able to smell the smells. Once I took a flower and put it to my lips, but then decided not to taste it because the flower was feeling pain, so I left it on its stalk and strode away.

I went to some of the animals such as chickens and cows and delighted in hearing the baby chicks peep as they ran after their mothers. I took pleasure in watching a new-born foal nuzzle its mother. I think my greatest pleasure was in watching the animals in a somewhat natural setting.

I would go to the nurseries in hospitals and look at the new-born babies. I was never allowed to hold one, for people did not know who I was, of course. I did not want to cause any problems and frighten anyone, but I was struck at how vulnerable the young are—not only the human baby, but also those in the animal kingdom. It was good for me to review this for it had been a long time since I had walked the Earth.

Then I decided I would visit war zones. I wanted to watch as the young soldiers fought. How did they fight? Did they fight with any love in their hearts or only anger and revenge? I was pleasantly surprised to note that many of the young men who had never killed before did so for the first time and had to grapple with their emotions.

They would put on a front for the rest of the unit, for one could not show what one was really feeling. Most were feeling great emotions of regret, sadness, and fear; and if they were religious, they felt they had sinned. They had been instructed and drilled and knew it was "kill or be killed." However, that did not help them when it actually happened, when they were across from an enemy who looked pretty much as they did. It was especially so when the uniform provided the only difference between two handsome young lads facing each other, both thinking "kill or be killed."

They did not know it, but I would walk between them and before they knew it, they had lost sight of the other one. But soon they had to kill. War is such a devastating choice. Those souls had their pre-birth agreements and knew this was how they were going to pass on. However, the physical part, the dying part, was difficult.

Many of the young men never regained normalcy. When they returned home, they did not know how to relate to others. They were quick to anger and used anger because they were so close to tears. Many of the young were broken. Then you see, if one of their close friends, or buddies as they were called, were killed, then there would be guilt as to why was it not me. How come I was spared?

Walking among them could be the young chaplains, many of them just out of seminary schools. There is a term, *they were not dry behind the ears*, and yet they had to comfort the soldiers. Many of them just used memorized platitudes, for they also were just scared and questioned their own calling many times.

Soldiers did not know that the angels were walking with them. The angels were not always seen, but they were there. If it were in that person's contract to not die on the battlefield, the angels were quite busy staving off the bullets, jamming the guns—anything to keep their young charge from dying.

It was a learning time for WW I and II, Viet Nam and the Korean war. These were learning times for all of us Angels. Now we have the Iraq war. Each war has gotten progressively more difficult for the young men and women to stay alive because of all the technologies and the new ways that they can be killed—the new weaponry of guns and tanks and bombs. Everything has changed.

As more youths were brainwashed, they would become the suicide bombers. Each war is progressively worse with young zealots blowing themselves up believing that it would bring them to Heaven quicker and they would live happily ever after according to their particular religion, which of course was not correct.

All religions have been distorted. Your religions are not correct. None of your religions are correct. People of the Islamic religion think that killing others and sacrificing themselves will bring them to Allah and provide them seventy virgins. We wonder when there is such a distortion how anyone could believe that lie. There are lies throughout all the religions. Most of you certainly believe that of the Christian religions, although the Fundamentalists try hard to accept everything verbatim.

This Channel was watching a program on television by a respected man whose name I will not disclose. He has a brilliant mind and memory and quotes many, many of the spiritual texts by memory. However, she was shocked to hear him condemn the other ministers and their churches for allowing the youths to hold dances. The touching between the man and woman, or the boy and the girl, could lead to moral misbehavior. That type of thinking belongs in the twelfth century! It is ridiculous to our minds and so the Word of Christianity goes on with each minister calling the other pastor down for his particular beliefs.

The Jews believe that their religion is *the* one, but it has so many antiquated parts to it that need revising. All those laws and rituals were valid long ago. Religions need to be brought to present time. They need to be modified and to bring in true spirituality. The examples that I have just mentioned are not true spirituality. There is fanaticism, the zealots, the Fundamentalists in all three of those religions.

As your world advances, it is coming to a time when there will be no religion, but just spirituality—the Ways of God, the open mindedness, the open heart, the Christ Consciousness, the Light, all of this in modern terms is Spirituality.

Your Space Brothers and Sisters exist and they exist in the highest level that they could possibly be. Ashtar chuckles over the term that he is referred to as an ET. He considers himself a spiritual Being. To him Earthlings are the ETs. When you reverse the concept, it is amusing.

People, open your hearts, open your minds. Change with the times. Do not grow stagnant with your ideas. You see, in our Angelic Realm, that is how we live. It is through the changes. We cannot become stagnant. We must always be changing . People who think they know Jesus and think that he is the same as yesterday need to understand that he is not! He has grown. Everyone must grow—men and women honing their trade and doing their soul's purpose. Everyone must change, dear people. Be open to new ideas and to receiving the Space Command.

I will close now. I AM Archangel Michael.

Well, we had a bit of a problem, eh? (Yes, I was so deep into trance that I just flipped the tape over forgetting that I needed to put in a new one.) But you see you already had transcribed that material so that there was no harm done. You just will transcribe what Michael has said and it will be fine. So we will stop now, for your energy is centered on the tape versus the channeling. (Yes, I know and I apologize for that.) There was no harm done, dear one. See you in a few days.

(Author's note: I suspect, Readers, you may feel as unfinished with this chapter as I do. I feel as if there is still a dangling carrot for us just out of reach. Forgive me!)

Your Space Brothers and Sisters Greet You

CHAPTER 11- CALIFORNIA BURNING

Good morning once again to our Readers and to this Channel. We have an exciting chapter on hand for you today—at least we think it is exciting. I now will step aside and let that person come forth. I will come back later, for I wish to make some comments on the California fires. (Thank you, Lord, I was hoping you would.)

Good morning friends and neighbors and I say *neighbors* for I do hope that you are with Me always. I have come once again to speak with you. **I AM your Father.** Some call me **Father God**; some call me **Christ Michael**; some call me **Aton.** I wear many hats.

I come to you this morning just for a short page or two, for I wish to comment on the fires that are burning in California. People are aghast at the fury of the fire elemental. What they see is a true Elemental in action. The fire elemental was called forth by the Earth Mother, for the changes have started, you see. This fire was to let you know what was to come. It is a cleansing.

It not only cleanses the underbrush, the density perhaps, but it cleanses the density of neighborhoods. There are so many houses built together—so many cabins built together. It is a cleansing and a warning to all of you that were involved. If your house was burned to the ground, take it as a gift from Mother Nature and do not condemn her. It is a gift given to you, for you did not lose your life, did you. You merely lost a possession.

Now you can step back and now you really have choices. Do you wish to rebuild? Or do you wish to move on and away from those areas. Those of you with higher

111

consciousness can you not see how this gift frees you up? It allows you to go out of the area, away where it could be safer for you.

Those of you that have read different material coming from the Internet, or books, or have listened to radio talk shows, know that the Earth changes are going to affect California a great deal; know that the ocean will be breaking on those shores ever further inland. We have said in a previous chapter (*Chapter 2*) that Malibu's shore line will be moved—perhaps a hundred miles or so inland.

When you think of it in those terms, it does not leave much land down there for the Los Angeles and San Diego areas, does it. It means that part of that land could be inundated from the ocean. Do you not see, People, the opportunity that is being given to you—what a wonderful gift that is being given to you? It is a gift of life. You did not lose your life, but merely your possession. Yes, there were choices as to what to grab as you were evacuating. Some grabbed family pictures, family histories. Others did not and regret it. Nevertheless, those were choices.

However, you can live with the fact that you still have a life, your children are safe. For many of you, your animals and pets are safe. It was not the *living* that Mother Earth was having attacked, it was density, the energy. This is a big hint to move on and to move away. Now some people may question as to what about the homes that were not touched? We say that that is that individual's karma.

There is karma there, a karmic reason for that person staying. Maybe that person later on down will decide to move, for he/she does not want to fight the anguish of fires and evacuation again. For many of them, this happened approximately four years ago and now this is a repeat performance. Do you not see the tremendous hint in that? You have your life for a second time. You lost your home for a second time. Do you not think that is a hint to get out? It has long been predicted to stay away from the coasts, as beautiful as they are.

This Channel loves the Pacific ocean with a passion and she used to walk its beaches and sing and chant as the waves crashed onto the shore. However, she does not live there anymore. She lives in Arizona and she knows that she will be moving around in that state also.

It is important, Readers, to listen to your souls — not to the personality/ego, not to the victim in you that is crying *oh,* using your particular expression, *oh shit, it has burned again!* No, it is a gift; it is a gift.

The fires will die down and as you have noticed there are always those dark ones that take advantage. Some were stealing the supplies, whatever they could find to steal. It even brought forth the arsonists who set some fires — the dark, you see. The dark always comes forth.

You have the television that gave excellent coverage on the fires. The people that were evacuated and went to the stadium, they had more commodities offered to them than they had ever partaken — acupuncture, massage, therapy, grief counselors, foods, diapers, formulas, sunscreen. All of this was free. How wonderful.

There were interpreters that gave of their time. How wonderful of the people who came forth. This is a test for you, those of you that have lost your homes. This is a test. Do not play the victim. It was set up in your pre-birth agreements. Your soul wanted to experience this. At the same time your soul said *now I will guide my body to leave the area.* However, some people are not in touch with their souls. It is their personality and they go into fear or into *woes me.* It is a hard task, but you asked for it.

There are no accidents; there are no exceptions. Your souls learned a great deal, but it is time to move on.

It is unheard of to have evacuated almost a million people successfully; it is unheard of. With these fires, that land could be compounded by earthquakes coming from the heat of the fires. It could trigger earthquakes. That whole area as beautiful as it is and was is to be reclaimed by Mother Earth and the elements, mainly by water.

Therefore, dry your tears, dry your tears and calm your fears, straighten your spine, make important conscious choices, follow your guidance, follow your souls. Do not act in haste but know in your heart that you are making the correct choice.

It is time to move on for those of you who have lived there or have relatives there and will share this book and this information with them. It is time to move on. People reading this book may know of people who are starting to rebuild, but it is time to move on. Listen to your souls. A prayer now and then to Me will not go un-noticed. I answer prayers that come from the heart. I do not answer prayers that come from ego. I do not answer prayers that come from victimization. I answer prayers that are heart-felt.

Therefore, Readers, I will leave you now and I bless you mightily. The people in that California area are mightily blessed by the angels and Masters and yes, even your Space Brothers. We are watching and helping this prelude of things to come. Picture those fires burning; picture what that would be like all over America—volcanoes going off and earthquakes happening, oceans roaring in. And yes, you could sit it out, wearing your masks, trying to breathe, but we are offering you a choice also to be lifted up and out and to watch all of that from the screens on our ships.

I will bless you and I will leave you now. I AM your God. Greetings. (*Thank you, God.*)

All right, dear one, we knew that something needed to be addressed with these fires—California burning. People needed a different perspective and if people would come out of fear and start thinking about it and to see that the objective of Mother Earth was not to kill anyone, but merely to remove them safely. And that was done with massive evacuation and with everything being given to them. Now do you not think that that was a miracle?

They had more given to them than if they had been living in their own homes. Is that not a miracle. Is that not a hint? I hope that people in southern California are questioning "why me?" That is a good place to start. "Why me? I lost everything but have my family and my pets and am well taken care of, but why me?" Maybe it was because you were meant to move to safer grounds—not to attempt to rebuild. If something has happened for the second time in approximately four years that is a pretty good hint. It is time to move on and to go to other greener pastures and stay away from the coasts.

Now unless you have anything else you would like to add to this, dear Channel, we will close up shop for the day. (No, Lord, I was hoping that someone would come forth and speak about this, for so many people are putting it in the term of "tragedy," which then makes it a victim statement. It is the soul's agreement, the soul's purpose to experience this and the soul's way of moving its body out, out and away.) I could not have said it better myself, dear one; so I will be back in a couple of days. Enjoy the Sheldan Nidle presentation of all the UFO information.

(10-27-07). We will all be there, you realize, looking over his shoulder.

Until later, blessings. (Thank you, Lord.)

CHAPTER 12- TUELLA'S REMARKS

(Author's note: I attended an all day workshop in the Phoenix area yesterday, October 27, 2007, presented by an excellent Emissary for spaceships. He has a phenomenal mind, more like a "walking Encyclopedia," and I have no doubt that he is a genius in his field of science and ET's. I have the greatest respect for his area of expertise. However, some of the material that he presented is different from what I have been given and it does leave me questioning as to what to believe.

Yeshua knew that I was questioning all of this so he brought back Lady Tuella who addresses some of the queries that perhaps you as a Reader may also be pondering.)

Dearest one, I am here. Now you wish to have a little side bar on this workshop. (Yes, please, Lord, I suspected that you would know I would.) Yes, of course, for his information does not always agree with what you have been given. (I know.) So what are your perplexities? (Well, according to this speaker, the whole evacuation of Earth is still on. The banking system has to change, then the lift-off will happen and everyone will be lifted off in a blink of an eye all by 2012 — in just four years. He has been on the ships, up there and down again, so it is very hard not to believe everything that he puts out there. He also shared a new map that shows that most of Arizona will be at the bottom of a huge lake that extends northward.

Yes, dear one, those are different perceptions aren't they? We have told you that Stasis is still a strong possibility, and we are not ruling that out. That proposal is still on the Council table.

He said that the Jupiter Effect would not happen, that it is not meant to be a sun and that Earth is not meant to have two suns. We say that it is a possibility—a strong possibility—and it is still on the Council table.

And we have told you that you are safe where you live. If Arizona is to be under a lake in four or five years, we would not have you living there. Why would people be moving to Colorado if a third of it was going to be a lake? So you see, dearest one, you have two differences of opinion here. It is up to you to make your own discernment.

You are not making this up, dear one. You are not projecting your ego onto the pages. You are not projecting your opinions onto the pages. And yes, this is coming through you telepathically, but at the same time there is no way that you could be making up what has been told to you. People have emailed you and told you how they love the energy of the books. If they love the energy, then there must be something that is right about the books.

It would be different if people could not feel the energy, but they do, and it is a loving energy since it is from us. It is from Source; it is from the Heavenly Spheres; and it is from me, Yeshua. So again, do not let that "doubting Thomas" of yours come forth! You have been told by Ashtar that evacuating the whole planet is not our reality. It will be given as a choice, But do stay with discerning, using common sense. So I think we will need to leave it there and just wait to see what the next four years will bring.

Approach this speaker's material, dear one, with discernment. He is a brilliant man—a genius—with very fine guides, very fine people who guide him. Even Lord Surea tells of the evacuations, but we consider them to be lift-offs by choice. However, we do not see everything that he says as happening. He just has a different perception from what we think is going to happen.

Now let us bring in another speaker and continue with the book. It is progressing nicely and this will be Chapter 12, I believe. It is time to bring back a woman, a Lady Master, and I will have her speak to you. (Thank you, Lord.) You are welcome. We will come back afterwards to speak to you. (All right, 10:20 AM.)

Good morning everyone on this fine Sunday, the 28th of October, close to Halloween, and on your way to celebrating the coming holidays. Many people refer to them as the *dreaded holidays,* yet each year everyone makes it through and has a wonderful time celebrating, feeling also relieved when it is all over. It is interesting that the last three months of a year are the hardest for people. Yet those months ought to be the ones that hold the most joy and celebrations.

I AM Tuella, back once again to continue where I left off. This Channel attended a workshop yesterday where much information was given to the participants in answer to their questions. *The speaker and his partner are dear souls, and I know them well.*

He described much about the Inner Earth, which I found delightful and informative, for we were all there at the workshop. He was accurate in his information since he has visited there. The Inner Earth is a phenomenal society—one that could be a prototype or a template for the civilization that lives on top of the Earth.

The speaker discussed evacuations and he sees that everyone will be evacuated. We do not. He sees all of the banking restructuring happening by 2012 and then after that the evacuation and after that the Earth changes.

TUELLA'S REMARKS

We see a slightly different sequence. We see that *perhaps* the banking will be restructured by 2012, but that is only four years from now. With humanity's being as it is and so influenced by the dark forces and deception, we cannot say for a certainty that the banking restructuring will be fully implemented or even begun by the year 2012.

You see we think of all of this still as in the realm of possibilities. There can be no time frame with possibilities. We do not see it as probabilities yet. It has not reached that point but is slowly getting there.

The banking changes could come first and then the First Contact. But again, we say that that could change. It is not necessarily lined up to happen that way. There could very well be First Contact and then the banking changes. Some see the lift-offs as a total evacuation. I do not. I think perhaps many will be lifted off after they have chosen to do so. On the other hand, there will be many who stick it out; try to stick it out; want to stick it out.

The lift-offs will be offered. The opportunities will come in waves with several months and perhaps a year in between. It gives time for people to adjust. They need time to adjust to something that is as large as this. Now it may so happen some of those who live further west and are in that lake region could perish. But that is their choice. They did not want to move. The map that was shared at the workshop shows Arizona at the bottom of a lake—the entire state. We do not know if that is true or not.

Gordon Michael-Scallion has Phoenix as a sea-port. We do not know if that is true or not. There certainly will be an encroachment of the waters into Arizona, but whether it is from a lake or an ocean, we do not know.

It is very difficult to predict things of this nature. Therefore, Readers, keep your discernment functioning at the highest level. There are messages running rampant on the Internet. Discern where the truth is. With some of it, you may just have to wait and see — wait it out, watch and see how it all is going to play out. We do not know it fully because so much enters into it. Humanity's way of taking action or taking no action plays into it. The Earth Mother's way of cleansing plays into it.

Now one could say that one could set up a particular scenario to happen and it could *exceed* one's expectations. More than you wished to happen could happen. Or it could be *less* than you had hoped it to be. I do not think that some of these predictions can be that precise.

The I Am America maps, the Gordon Michael-Scallion maps and now this new map each show a different scenario, a different world. Is that not interesting? These have come from exceptionally conscious Beings, high level Beings and yet all three of them have put out a different map. Therefore, somewhere in between there is what will happen.

Some people will say, *well I think I will go with the worst scenario and if it does not happen, so much the better.* Some will say *we will just stick it out and go with the least changes of the scenarios.*

The workshop presenter does not plan to leave California. He does not see it as breaking up as predicted on *Gordon Michael-Scallion's map.* But on this new map, the Rocky Mountains have disappeared. However, according to him, as we heard yesterday, we will all be safely on the ships! Humanity will be safely on the ships and then all the Earth changes will happen. Then Arizona can be under the lake that will be formed. Then Lemuria and Atlantis can rise.

TUELLA'S REMARKS

These are interesting times, Readers, very interesting times—times when you will need to not go into fear but to know that you *will* be guided as to where to go, what to do. Trust in your guidance.

There could be many of you who do not realize that you are being guided. Yet you have the saying, *I have this gut feeling.* Therefore, they go with their gut. Now *that* is guidance, and the soul puts it into the gut for them. Follow your guidance, dear Readers. When you receive this book, you will then have a fourth scenario where some of it may happen and some of it may not—where evacuation is a choice that we call a *lift-off* and others call it a total evacuation.

Use your discernment. This is really a game plan of *wait and see*, isn't? Live your life in the moment; work your purpose; earn your money; pay your bills; pay your taxes, giving to Caesar what is Caesar's for tax time will be coming up soon. Cast your vote for the candidate of your choice and live your life in the Christ Consciousness. That is all you can do; that is all that is being asked of you—to be a walking Christ who is love and consciousness, shedding your Light codes wherever you plant your feet.

Keep walking; keep talking love; keep being love; keep acting love. And as that saying goes, *let the chips fall where they may.* Follow your gut feeling. If you feel like you will be lifted up, you will. If you feel like you won't, you won't. If you feel like you will move, you will. If you feel like you won't, you won't. But live your life in consciousness.

That is all I wish to say, dear Readers, may you forever walk with God in full consciousness.

I AM Lady Tuella.

TUELLA'S REMARKS

Well, dear Readers, you have three maps to gaze at with each one being different. Who to believe? It is truly up to you. That is all, dear one, I bless you for today. We will start afresh in a couple of days. (All right, thank you, Lord.) You are welcome. (10:10-10:50 AM on 10-28-07)

CHAPTER 13- YESHUA REMINISCES

*Good morning once again, Readers, and to this Channel. Blessed are the peacemakers... **I AM Yeshua**, and I come to you today somewhat heavy in my heart, for we see the struggle of the Light with the dark and, while the Light will travail, it is sad for us to see how the dark can manipulate the thoughts of men and women—how they can become puppets instead of following their own soul's Light.*

*(Author: it was at this point that Yeshua just kept on dictating. I knew then that he was the Presenter. Therefore, I just changed the font to regular print. At the end he had blended into **The Many,** since they rarely come alone.)*

It astounds us that this can be so. And yet when humanity has dropped or lowered its consciousness throughout its many lifetimes, it is difficult to not come back into the same pattern. It is difficult to rise above all of that, for when you come back in for a new lifetime, you come in at the level where you were when you left the previous lifetime.

Just because you died, you are not promoted, although it would be a very nice thought. You come back to the same trials and tribulations that you undertook before. This time, however, you may find that solutions may come more rapidly and you may have more *ah-ha's* than you had before.

People, if you only knew how futile it is to commit suicide. Many of the terrorists have done this but they have distorted aspects of their religion. It is so futile because you come back almost instantly to the same problems that you had tried to avoid. Many times the problems have multiplied with intensity. One could say that they become exponential.

Each time you do not address particular problems and try to avoid them by killing yourself, you come back to find that those problems have developed exponentially into a greater and greater problem.

I, **Yeshua**, am speaking to you this morning for much has been going on on your planet, not only in America, but worldwide. America has had its problems and is having its problems with a government that is totally out of control—a government that ought to never have been put in power (the election was stolen, as you know)—to the point where America has lost her dignity.

There are few people throughout the world who respect her for her integrity. They respect the amount of money that she is able to accrue—much through unethical means. However, they no longer respect her as one to follow, as the *big father* to whom they can bring their problems.

Isn't it unfortunate that people who wish to relocate in America do so mostly because of the better economic conditions? Is it not sad that they do not wish to come for the laughter and joy and the freedom of thought that was once allowed? These freedoms are being taken away from the citizens of America. They are being infringed upon step by step.

Again it is the dark ones manipulating, taking a perverse joy in how they can break a person; send a person to prison; strip a person of his or her dignity; relieve a person from office because he no longer would continue telling the lies that was required of him. He no longer served a purpose, you see. Is it not sad that people do not

126

wish to come to America for its honesty and its integrity? However, we are speaking of the different levels of mentality of different dimensions, are we not?

Those of you who have read the fourth book, *Realities of the Crucifixion*, know that in my days as Jesus, the dimensions were much lower. The mentality, the consciousness was much lower. They did not have anyone to turn to but their priests in their particular religions and many times, just as it is now, those priests were *puppets of darkness.*

Humanity has grown up, has matured throughout the years. But it has not grown that much with integrity. It has matured because of the—how shall we put it—the kicks in the ribs, or in the stomach, or in the backside that it has received over the centuries. When you are down, are you not kicked like a dog? That is the way it was in those ancient days.

They stoned the people and then when they were down, they kicked them. Back in the days of the witch-hunts, who was the authority—the priests, those who thought they had all the answers. Only God the Father has all the answers, my beloveds—only God the Father has the answers.

He has gradually been showing you His different *hats.* If there can be different aspects of you, do you not think that there could be different Aspects of God the Father? Of course, for He is known by many names. In this book He is known as Christ Michael, Aton, and Hatonn. There are other names. Each one carries a specific personality, just like it does with you.

Do you not think that you act differently at times? Now I am not talking about a *split personality* as the psychologists might be suggesting at this time. Those

127

multiple personalities come about when people have been abused—usually sexually abused. Then a different personality springs forth. But those are not the personalities to which I am referring. I suppose one could say they are aspects of your ego.

There are people who are entirely different when they are at parties. They can be very loud and get drunk and are different from the way they are in the work place, where they are all business and authoritative. That is another aspect of their ego. If they are a loving Being at home, they will be the loving father and loving husband, another aspect of the ego.

Down throughout the ages your Father has shown Himself also in different ways. However, His core is pure Love and pure Light—all of which you have in your bodies. With the help of His warrior friend, Sananda, He made His body that I, Jesus, occupied. Actually, it was Sananda who was walking in the body, but he was named Jesus.

We learn so much when we take a body, for so much more can be experienced. When you are in Heaven, how can you experience anyone hating you? Everyone loves everybody. But take a body and oh my, do you ever experience hate! Do you know what it is like when someone hates you and you feel that energy? You think about it for days. You ponder, *why does he hate me? Why does he hate me? I have done nothing to him.* That is just the point, you see, for many times that hatred comes from jealousy which is another dark aspect.

When I was your Jesus, I experienced much hatred and I would turn to my three Marys, whom I have told you about—the Marys of my heart—my Mary Magdalene, my Mother Mary, my Mari-am, my adopted cousin-sister. All

128

three of them also experienced the energies of hatred, you see, just as you have in this lifetime.

You can feel when people do not like you. It seems to be especially so in the teenage years, those years that are so difficult, those years where you think you know everything and your parents know little (*chuckles*). And if you are a male, the fuzz is just starting on your cheeks and you stroke it and can hardly wait until you have a full beard, for then you will feel like a man.

In this day and age if you have a beard, you may find that it is more trouble than it is worth, for you are always having to trim it to get it to the length that you prefer. Then your hands always stroke it. Men stroke their beards when they are thinking.

Our dear Readers, now is a time of great strife in your lives. Many of you are aware of the different predictions from the Mayan calendar, the Hopi Indians, Nostradamus, your religions—all are projecting the *End Times*. Now what does the End Times mean for each one of you? I will tell you emphatically, it does not mean the end of your world! But it does mean a beginning—a new birth. In esoteric teachings, we have the life and death cycles. It does not mean that you are going to die. It just means that when you are finished with something; you end cycle. You close the door so that a new rebirth can take place.

Just know, dear friends, that it is up to you to make a new beginning. When we speak of the *new beginnings,* we are speaking about the spaceships. It is up to you to decide whether you wish to have a new beginning on a spaceship. The ships are coming, dear people, the ships are coming. Know that they will be landing; know that you will be welcomed aboard; know that you will have choices to make. You will have choices as to whether to go into fear, or to go into joy—to receive or to reject; to attack or to hold out your hand in friendship. These are all choices. We will all greet you. Often many of you have wondered what a Master looks like. Well, you will soon know. Many of you may have wondered how a Master sounds when he talks; what does he look like when he is dressed in his finery? You will soon find out.

Receive us in joy and love, for that is how we will come to you—with joy and love and with arms upraised in greetings. Receive us, dear friends.

I AM **The Many** today. I speak for **The Many**. Greetings!

All right, dear one, let us call this thirteenth chapter, Reminiscing. *We think this will do it for today. We believe that the recorder was able to record this even though low on batteries. See you in a few days. Good day. (Thank you, Lord, good day.)*

(Author's note: Even though I am channeling, my intuition and/or guide is still active. I got the feeling to take a sneak peek at the recorder light to see if it was still glowing brightly. Might have known; it was not. Therefore, I knew I had but a limited time to record all of what Yeshua was saying. I told him this while he was speaking, and he assured me that his words were recorded and would be all right. However, the chapter would have to be brought to a close soon, which is what he graciously did. Nevertheless, I always feel as if he might have said more if the circumstances had been different. Alas, the woes of channeling and recording...)

CHAPTER 14-NADA- LOVE, PEACE, LIGHT

Good morning once again everyone on this bright and sunny day in Arizona. There are some who predict that Arizona will be at the bottom of a lake! Shall I say to just wait and see (chuckles)? We still think that other things will happen first. You do not have to be afraid. That is why the lift-offs are being offered to you.

Well, I come this morning with joy in my heart. I have been reading the chapters right along with this Channel, and we are very pleased with the work. We always chuckle, for when she is through reading a chapter she will say, oh, this is not half bad! *Of course she is referring not only to the material, but to the fact that she was able to channel it.*

Those of you who have tried it and only were able to hear a word or a sentence or two know that this is quite a feat. Have you ever sat down and tried to write a 200 page book with every word channeled? Sometimes she does not give herself enough credit for what she has accomplished. We are quite pleased.

This morning we are going to have somewhat of a change of subject matter here, for the last couple of chapters have been really intense—with the California fires and the chapter on evacuations. Let us approach another subject. When was the last time that you thought about what Love means? When was the last time that you thought about what Peace means? When was the last time that you thought about what being a Lightweaver means?

We are going to bring in a Speaker who will address those subjects and then tie them in with the theme of this book. Without further remarks from me, I will step aside and let her speak.

Hello once again everyone. **I AM Lady Nada,** back to give you a few words of wisdom and to bring you some joy. My Flame was telling you about the subjects for this morning: Love, Peace, and Light.

Let us start with Love, for if you do not have Love, you will not have Peace. And if you do not have Peace, you will not have Light. They are all three connected, you see. Of course we could bring in Joy, Compassion, Receiving, and all of those other elements that make up the Christ Consciousness.

Commander Korton has spoken a bit about Love in the Introduction chapter on Communication. He told you that Love has many aspects to it. It seems as if love is somewhat *bi-polar* in itself in that it can be endearing and loving, a beautiful energy. Then if it is not used correctly, people think of it as possessive, jealous, controlling, not caring, demanding. Does that sound like any of your lovers, Readers?

Is it not sad that they call that *love?* Or, they even may not call it anything. If you are married, isn't it a given that you are in love? People do not realize that love needs to be nurtured like a garden—watered with tears of laughter, joy, and endearment. Love must be physical in hugs and kisses and nuzzling around the ears—sweet kisses over your eyes. That is a part of love.

I am not going to put it into the physical sense of sexual touching, for so often that can turn into lust and that is not love. That is being in the lower centers, while love, true love, is in the heart—the deep inner chambers of your heart. You have two sections of the heart chakra and it is the sacred inner chamber, the one that you approach from your back, where you find true love. Love is energy. It holds the Light. They correlate. How much love you are able to hold in that body correlates to how much Light you are able to hold onto.

Every person on this planet down through the ages, down through antiquity, needs love, is love, seeks love, exploits love, denigrates love. Do you not think that when you are abusing love, that you are not abusing your Heavenly Father? He is pure love and He has given a Cell of Himself to you. He is in your body—in the cells of your body. All you have to do is to connect to it. It is in your heart chakra. All you have to do is to connect to it.

When you have that love, dear friends, do you not have Peace? People, think back on your teen years, those dreaded years of high school where the peer pressure is so great—the pressure to conform to everyone else's ideals of how to behave, what to wear, what to say, what music to listen to. It is a time when the hormones are rampant. It is the time when a boy and girl are actually seeking their mate.

Eons ago young women were married in their teens—teenage years. The men were usually older, for they had their apprenticeship or education to finish. They had to earn their wives. They had to hold positions of prominence, or positions where they could support a wife in order to earn her dowry! Some of those ancient customs are still practiced in Europe today and even in South America, where marriages are arranged and come with a dowry.

But how controlling that is—the man has bought his wife and she has given him her money and estates. Many hundreds of years ago the young Royals would be frivolous and go through their wives' money, usually spending it on

133

fancy clothes and jewelry. Consequently, there was not much peace in those marriages, for there was not the true love. There came a time when the Ancestors would raise up their hands in frustration because of the indiscretions down through the generations.

Where is peace? There is no peace when you are making war. All of those soldiers have little to none, for they are in fear most of the time. Those of you who are in the military have no peace in your hearts. You are heavily controlled. You love and then you control your spouse. But there is always that underlying fear, for when you are attacked you must fight back. Very few people in the military have peace in their hearts.

Peace is synonymous with love. When you carry a great deal of love and Light, you also carry peace. Peace has its own dark side, shall we say, the opposite side, the duality, for if there is not peace there is war. If there is not peace, there is bickering, back-stabbing, gossiping. Again there is not much love and therefore, there is not much peace.

What does it take to be a Lightworker, a Light-weaver—one who weaves patterns of Light, love and peace together? It takes consciousness. It takes a growing Christ Consciousness. *Blessed are the peacemakers...* as our Lord once said. It takes consciousness, for those of you who have studied long and hard, and I do not mean in the religious sense, but have studied esoteric literature, the lessons that the Masters give to their chelas.

Masters overlay their Light on their special students. When I say *special,* it means that that student is full of Light and love and is deserving of his or her Master's overlighting.

This Channel is overlighted by your Lord Yeshua. She is overlighted by Saint Germain. And now this Channel is overlighted by that great Commander Ashtar. He has taken her under his wing and has given her her former hat to wear, for she too is a Commander and has been for eons of time in the Star Fleets. She is a Lightweaver.

She weaves Light as she transcribes these books. These books are full of love, Light, and peace. When you read them, that is what you feel. When a Lightweaver is around you, that is what you feel. You feel warmth and appreciation, and you feel that you are not judged. A Light weaver is so full of Light that when walking the Earth, the person is planting encodements of Light into the planet. It actually helps the planet's grids to stay strong when there is so much Light showered upon them.

The California fires brought people together in unprecedented numbers. It brought out camaraderie, fellowship, caring. It brought out many attributes that people carry in their hearts. It re-lit the attributes that people had not been using lately. It was a heavy time for many. However, as we have said in other books, many times when dramatic changes come, that is when the physical bodies evolve the most.

Most of them spiral up and they step on another rung of the ladder of evolution. It brings out the best in them. It re-kindles the love cell in them, the peace, and it brings them more Light. I dwell with my Flame, the Lord Sananda, on his mother ship, the New Jerusalem, that was anchored by the Lady Tuella and others when she had her Earth life. It is anchored in a higher dimension over the Yucatan and is so huge that it covers much of the Gulf of Mexico. That ship is anchoring the Light for humanity for this southern part of the United States. These huge mother ships do not rotate that much but are lowered through different dimensions and then finally anchored in where they will stay for eons of time—until it is again time to move. You see, we too pack up and move at times (*chuckles*).

Lightweavers, this is what is needed on the planet today. Instead of spending billions on destructive wars, why not spend billions on turning young adults into Light-weavers, teaching them about love, peace, and Light. It ought to be part of a school's curriculum, the teaching of the wisdom of the Masters.

There is so much lacking in the schools' education systems. They take out *prayer;* they take out the *pledge of allegiance to the flag.* What do they replace it with? Dogmatism and tired old history that is not accurate. The dogma that they are teaching you in a religious school or university is not accurate either. You graduate, having memorized religious stanzas, religious platitudes, but it is what you have asked for. It is where your soul has led you.

You see, changes must come to those types of universities. Changes must come to your school systems, for unless someone starts changing the habitual curriculum, it will be taught over and over and over. It becomes a *cookie cutter*—the young adults who come out of those schools are the result of cookie cutters.

Do they carry peace? *NO.* Are they a Light-weaver? *Some are.* Do they carry love? *Some do.* But most teaching, you see, is so mixed up with religiosity that it becomes, what I would term, somewhat *gooey*—the gooey type of Christianity. They teach lies and make so much of the fact that our beloved Lord was crucified. They make so much of the fact about the blood. It is so *erroneous,* yet they will not listen because you are taking away a cultural belief and they will not listen.

136

Love, Peace, and Light all are connected—all intertwined, all mistreated, all misjudged, all miscalculated. People question and do not get the answers; or, I will say, the correct answers. So much of the information is skewed.

There is not much more that I can say, except it is our prayer for you that you will let us into your hearts, that you will let the ships land and receive us, so that we can teach you what true spirituality is. You can visit our libraries and YES, we have libraries on the ships. You can visit our libraries, watch the video of the holographic dramas right in front of your eyes. If you want to visit ancient Roman times, the amphitheaters, you can be there. But I imagine most of you will head right to the libraries to read about and experience *Jesus*.

This Channel has said to a friend, *I am immediately going to go to the library when I come aboard ship*! She was so much a part of that biblical life, you see. And she is still wanting the truth about it, to see it. In those libraries you can be a part of it again in a holographic way, so that you will feel it, sense it. She wants to feel the emotions of that time. She wants to visit her past life as Mariam, Yeshua's cousin-sister. She wants to know what went wrong. *Why wasn't God's body able to override the evil of those days?* She wants those answers, just as all of you do.

Therefore, when you are invited aboard our ships, go to the libraries, read and become part of the drama to your heart's content. Know and feel what true love, Light, and peace are all about. We offer this to you. It is our *carrot* to you. We offer you the carrot of our libraries. Come to us. We will be awaiting you.

Greetings, I AM Lady Nada.

Your Space Brothers and Sisters Greet You
NADA – LOVE, PEACE, LIGHT

(Oh, thank you Lady Nada; it is always so informative.) You are welcome, dear child; you are welcome.

All right, my dearest Flame and confidant has spoken once more. (Yes, she is always a joy to listen to.) So, dear one, type it up and I will see you in a couple of days. (Lord, when are we going to have the title of the book?) I will give you the title the next time we meet. (All, right, thank you.) All for now, dear one, with blessings. (Thank you, Yeshua, 10:30 AM.)

CHAPTER 15- DIVINE MOTHER

Good morning everyone, I AM Yeshua, coming forth to bring you our next chapter. We are very pleased with how this book is progressing, and we give our thanks to the various Presenters for coming forth and giving their words of wisdom—all of which I know you Readers are gobbling up and wanting more.

This morning it gives me great delight to bring forth another one of our women Presenters—a woman you have heard from in the past and is always a part of our books. I will let her speak next.

Good morning everyone, it is so nice to be back once again. I think I will let my name be a surprise for now. Many of you know me from biblical times, but you do not know me for the person I am today. I was the Mother of your Lord, but I do not wish to speak of that ancient era, for we are all evolving together. **I AM** the **Divine Mother** of all!

I have graduated also and have gone up that ladder of evolution in my own way. We will call it the *Cosmic evolution* or the *Heavenly evolution,* for I am no longer a part of Earth, you see. I come many times in your prayers to help you. Many ask me and still think of me as the *end all* of their problems. However, it really is not I. It is your Father. He is the one to whom you should bring your problems.

Now why have I come this morning? I come with joy in my heart, for we are ever approaching your new world. Now I am not particularly speaking of a new planet, but a new way of being—a new consciousness. We chuckle as this Channel talks to her daughters with her different ideas. They make note that *oh, that's Mom's world*. This is how I am coming to you this morning, for I am talking about our new world. All of you Readers and all of you Lightworkers, today is our new world, is it not? It will be one that will be full of Light. The darkness will have dissipated somewhat. However, there will be those who will be lighting up the dark side of themselves still, and that must be transmuted.

Therefore, not everything will be—you have that expression, *wine and roses*—not everything will be of the highest order, for this is evolution and not everyone is on the same rung of the ladder! However, it is a beautiful time that is coming forth for everyone, this beautiful world that you all will be making—this new consciousness that you will be entering into, full of laughter and joy, beautiful energies, shimmering energies, energies that have no name, colors that have no name. And I will add, *as yet*, for you will find a new vocabulary for them and put words to them.

Just look at how your English language has changed over the years. There are many different words you have brought into being, for you now have computers to work with. Do you think you would have used the word *download* fifty years ago? I am *downloading* this and *deleting* that. Did you ever think you would be talking like that?

So you see, with every growth there comes new vocabulary. New dictionaries have to be written to hold the new words. In your voting machines you have the *hanging chads*. Did you have that years ago? NO. So everything progresses and everything moves forward in this new world that you are all helping to create. There will be many changes and you will help to create all of them.

Now, am I aboard the ships? Of course I am. I do not stay permanently but I do come and go. I come in my Light body and put in my *two-cents-worth,* as the expression goes.

We are very active on board the ships. We do not just sit and chit-chat. If there is a reason to come aboard, we do so. We follow protocol. We are business-like and we work. We are working with the energies of humanity.

Many times I go to the library because I want to see a particular time in history. I visit that era to see if there could have been a different way to solve that particular problem. One of the darkest times was during the Inquisition—the Spanish Inquisition. The priests, fathers of the church, held court and held a person's life or death in their hands. It was their decision whether someone had blasphemed, had been a traitor to God's work.

When you look back on it, Readers, is it not amazing that humanity put itself in such a predicament that just a handful of the religious sect could make or break you—could condemn you? Many times they were putting someone to death who was of a higher consciousness and had said things, perhaps foolishly, that were beyond the comprehension of most people.

It was a dismal time in history. I would visit these times, you see, and study them. What could we have done differently? What could I have done? They had statues of me and they prayed to me and they asked me to absolve their sins after they had condemned someone to death. They asked me in their dark righteousness to absolve them, to cleanse them and make them pure again, so that they could turn around the next day and do it all over again!

People prayed to God the Father and to the Holy Spirit, the feminine side of God—although religion today

141

still wants to put her into the masculine gender and the Fundamentalists repeatedly call the Holy Spirit, *Him*—this feminine side of God. They prayed to Jesus to absolve their sins and they prayed to me.

As you have surmised by now, **I AM** known as **Mother Mary** and that was a difficult time of life. But you see, what I am telling you is that as difficult as those biblical times were, the times of the Spanish Inquisition were equally hard. While I was not present in the flesh, I was there (*spiritually*) simply because the people called upon me so many times.

I am always there when people say my name but many times all I can do is send them Light and love, for it is up to them to find their own peace. They will find their peace only when there is no darkness in their heart. However, they do not know this. Many times the innocent of the lower economical strata, the old women sages, the grandmothers who stroked the babies had more love and peace in their hearts. They wore home-spun clothes and had little to eat, but they could still croon and hold the babies. I then would be with them!

I would shed peace on their hearts then, for you see I could come to them and through them because they had the innocence of a child. They had the innocence of those babies who were happy, for they knew no difference. They were loved and they knew no difference. It was not until they got older and realized how hard life was for them that they lost that innocence.

And yes, for those of you who are into New Age thought and knowingness, those souls chose to experience those lifetimes. However, that did not make it any easier for them. Remember, when you choose a lifetime, you also *choose to forget* what you had been previously! You could be a Master crawling around the floor of a little thatch-roofed hut—a Master who came in to experience the poverty.

Do you not think that during those Elizabethan times, those times that you will find in the stories written by the different authors, those ancient times of England, the rich in their carriages and the urchins in the streets— Charles Dickens became famous for his novel *Christmas Carol* with Scrooge. There are many Scrooges in the world—that I was not there? I was there.

Readers, be aware that as you climb the rung of your particular ladder to consciousness that you had many of those types of ancient past lives, not only during the biblical times where perhaps you were in the crowd, watching and listening as that glorious son of mine gave his series of Beatitudes that are spoken to this day. *Blessed are they... Blessed are they...* he would say.

I say to you, blessed are you for going forward, for sticking it out, for the times ahead will be most difficult. However, you all signed up for them with such joy. Not everyone, you see, was able to come to Earth and be a part of this great last drama, bringing the world into her next dimension. You wanted to be a part of this drama where spaceships will land, where you will see wonders that you have never seen before—wonders that are only in science fiction books—and where you will be able to touch the hands of the Masters and touch the robes of the Goddesses and marvel at their beauty.

What you will be seeing is the perfection, the perfection of what to look like when you are a God in your own right. This Channel is in tears, for she feels my energy. I have come very close to her. I love her dearly; I hold her in the deepest respect, as I hold each one of you.

DIVINE MOTHER

Dearest Readers, open your hearts more. As you read these pages, feel the love that I am pouring out onto them; feel the energy, for I am within these pages. The time has come when the rose-colored glasses must be taken off, when the shades, the blinders must be taken off your eyes. The time has come when you must see clearly; see the world for what it is right now. See the changes going on. See the darkness rise and be transmuted. Note the lies that are coming forth.

Those of you who listen to the news or read the papers, know that some of it is true and some of it is a lie. However, when you watch the local news on television and see or hear of the local murders, the different acts of violence that go on, know that everything is rising to the top so that it can be skimmed off, skimmed off and transmuted.

We shine our Light onto the world. It is continuous. Feel us. Love us; love us back as we love you. Love in that pure clean way that has no religiosity in it and no dogma in it—just pure spirituality and the love of humanity and the love of God. If you can love God and then love yourself, you will have no problem in rising ever upward.

You will have no problem in welcoming us when we come forth. I too shall walk out of the doors of a landed spaceship. I too shall come!

Blessings to all God's children. I AM known as your Divine Mother, the Mother of your Lord. Greetings.

(Thank you so much, it is a beautiful chapter.) You are welcome, my precious one. Your lifetime with me was not our only time together. We had other times; we had other times.

Your Space Brothers - Sisters Greet You
DIVINE MOTHER

All right, dear one, that was our Mother, a hard act to follow, so I too will say, Greetings. (Thank you, Yeshua. 10:15 AM, 11-03-07.)

Your Space Brothers and Sisters Greet You

CHAPTER 16- DJWHAL KHUL- DEATH

Good morning blessed ones—our Readers and this Channel—I am back once again to continue our most interesting book. We are zooming through this book, like we do most of them, one chapter after the other. This Channel is keeping up with the typing, for she is always ready when the next "sitting" approaches.

There has been death in many of your families as of late. These transitions are difficult for the people who are left behind. Sometimes they are difficult for the souls who are leaving, but usually it is difficult for those who are left afterwards, after the funeral, to pick up the pieces and to continue living.

In the years from now to 2012 and even beyond, humanity will be experiencing one death after another. The reasons are many and varied. For some it is just time for the body to die or for the soul to progress. For others it is a transition that they have requested They do not wish to be a part of the changes that will be occurring.

They do not wish to be confronted by spaceships and spacemen. They do not believe in Masters. Therefore, they are saying "get me out of here." And there will be many such reasons for death. They will be rubber-stamped "Requests Filled."

We have a tremendous Being who will be speaking to you this morning. He is very familiar with life and death, for he walked your Earth as a man who experienced death many times. He is known throughout the esoteric community for his literature and his writings. Without further words from me, I will let him come forth. I will then come back and give you the title of this book, dear one. (Thank you, Lord.)

Good morning everyone, **I AM** known as **Djwhal Khul**. (*Hello, I have not heard from you for quite some time.*) Yes, it is good to be back. I probably am best known as the **Tibetan** speaking about *Rays and Initiations*. However, the information continues. It continues from the time that I was using that great Channel, Alice Bailey, and bringing forth her many books. I have not found such a Channel since, for she was astounding in her ability to bring through that information.

Those books were quite intricate. They were pedantic. They were hard to understand and to decipher. Consequently, I will speak more simply for this book. In fact I have spoken before in this Channel's previous book (*Book FIVE, Messages from the Heavenly Hosts.*)

When your Lord asked me to be a part of this book, I was not quite sure what I was going to speak about. However, when there was a death in this Channel's extended family, I thought that now was the time to speak about *death* and its transitions.

As with anything else, there are so many religious ideas around death. The church fathers have made a good rendition (*facetiously implied*) of telling people what death is like. And their words or dogma are not always necessarily true.

Death is a transition. It is stepping from one dimension into another. There are different deaths as you know. There can be violent deaths from a shooting, or "accidental death" by a car crash. There can be lengthy illnesses, such as multiple sclerosis which is a slow, progressing death. There can be deaths from illnesses such as cancer where the cells multiply in an unhealthy way.

Each death, you see, is an experience set up by the soul. Perhaps the soul wanted the experience of what it would be like to die after having been shot. It wanted an experience to know what it would be like to die in a car crash. It wanted the experience of a long, debilitating illness. It wanted to know what it would be like to fight the battle of cancer.

Those souls that have more awareness when it comes to the time when their body is riddled with cancer will just step through that door without any hesitation. Now that does not mean that their bodies do not register any fear, because that stems from ancient times—the ancient brain-stem that signals to stand, fight, or flee.

If a person with cancer decides that he or she is not going to live through that illness, that person makes the correct choice to not subject himself to months of chemotherapy and/or radiation therapy. It is not necessary. How many of you know people who battled for so long and then died anyway?

However, before we jump to any judgments about the soul's wanting that experience, we need to remember that there is a tremendous learning experience when someone has radiation or chemotherapy. One must fight his/her own demons, the fears. Some people become claustrophobic as they lie there in an isolated room since no one else can be with you when you are receiving the rays of radiation. You hear the groaning and grinding of the machine. You then have to battle with the radiation burns that can cause the skin to slough off in large patches.

The treatments for cancer can have further repercussions. They can wipe out small percentages of your brain. They can affect the swallowing mechanism of your throat. Even though it was only the breast area that was supposed to receive the ray, other areas can also be affected. (*Chemotherapy has other drastic side effects such as vomiting and hair loss and great debilitation.)* Consequently, there are tremendous learning experiences available to the soul. When the body dies, the soul takes this experience Home with it.

Now, you have probably heard that the soul simply will step into another dimension at the moment of death. That is true to such an extent that sometimes the person does not know that he or she has died. That person will carry on with life not realizing that he/she is dead. It becomes a weird situation, for there is a lack of awareness in the soul. There can be a funeral or memorial service and the soul still does not know it is dead.

Then after a certain length of time, even six weeks or more, the soul catches on. *Hey, something is not quite right here. I wonder if I am dead?* The soul starts speaking to those nearby. They turn out to be the angels that are watching over the soul. Then the person is taken to different areas that are, shall we say, in Heaven or Nirvana. The person is then instructed and reviews his or her past life.

Other souls are somewhat unconscious when they cross over. They are asleep. They are taken to a healing area and are watched over and left to sleep while they are healing their etheric body.

Death is a wonderful transition, but in the physical world, your body is either alive or dead, there is *life or death.* In the Heavenly spheres, there is only *life.* Souls wake up and they are alive, vibrantly alive. They see the joy around them. They feel the love. They meet their family members and hear their stories once again. There are always angels assigned to them. They are never alone, just as they had angels to guide them in their physical life.

They have angels who watch over them and guide them in their heavenly life.

Now I am not going to speak about the lower levels that so many Christians call *hell*, places where there is no Light. You who read these books would not even buy them if you were not constantly evolving into the Light.

Death is a beautiful experience. It is full of Light and the sound of rushing waters and the sounds of Heavenly music. Whatever your spiritual belief, there will be a person to greet you. Do not be afraid of death, dear ones. Do not go into depression and long days of grieving and mourning. And yes, do grieve but let it be a natural grieving because your body is missing the person. However, that will pass. Let it pass. Do not hang on to it.

After a certain length of time, go through the closet and recycle the clothes. Do not keep things of that nature. It is time to let them go. Some families are in such strife with each other that there is fighting right up to the end. There is fighting with the will. There is fighting with greed regarding who will get the money.

There needs to be forgiveness in the heart. If you did not approve of one who died, forgive that person. Forgive that person for judging, for you do not know what that person's spiritual circumstances are or what the spiritual agreements were. Pre-birth agreements are set up determining how a person is going to die. Many people will choose cancer because it is quite an explosive type of death that releases the soul quickly. It can be quite a scary time, for cancer seems to sound a death-knell for people.

One of these days, or shall we say centuries, people will not be afraid of death. They will lay a tired body down, close their eyes, take some deep breaths, and the next thing they know, they will be in another dimension while their body is peacefully stilled. They will joyfully be greeting everyone. They will be full of Light and happiness.

Now there are areas in the Heavenly spheres where souls can go to be healed, for they have traveled in their etheric body which could be ravaged also from the death of the physical body. Those etheric bodies need to be healed. It is done with music, Light, chanting, crystals, and colors. This all brings healing to the etheric body. The death scars need to be erased. Otherwise, they would bring cancer back in with them for the next life and die again from that illness—again and again. If those death scars are erased each time, they can die in different ways. Or they can choose it all over again.

Just know, Readers, that even though your death has ravaged the body, whether in car crashes where you have lost limbs or even your head, or by a debilitating illness, all of this is repaired. Now in this present lifetime, if you had been decapitated in the previous life, you may suffer from headaches or immobility of the neck that had stemmed from the previous life's death—the *death game*, we call it.

Everything that you have thought about concerning death has also been addressed in Heaven, or Nirvana—everything. If you have wondered whether a loved one will meet other loved ones, do you not think that this has been addressed and planned? If people have been married twice, they may worry about meeting their different spouses as they make their transitions. All is well. These were agreements.

Any jealousy or feelings of that nature are all on the physical plane. When you pass on, you will see your different husbands or wives and have no feelings of animosity toward them whatsoever! You will remember your agreements. All of those dark emotions, you see, are of the physical plane. When you drop your body, you drop those dark emotions also. Now we are talking about souls of Light. Of course there can be the dark souls that carry their dark thoughts forward. However, we are not speaking about that. We are speaking about the transition that humanity will make. There will be drownings, injuries from earthquakes with subsequent deaths. All of this was foreseen as you sat and talked with the others members of your life's game plan. All of this was foreseen and how you would play it out was discussed.

For those of you who are left behind, rejoice in the passing of your loved one. Let your body grieve; yes, but remember there is that part of you—that knowingness, that wisdom in you—rejoice, for all is well. All is truly well! The souls are happy. They are relieved that they have passed that life-time examination. They may have years before they will have to think about another life and a subsequent death.

Most souls are eager to progress. They are eager to evolve. Consequently, they are eager to take another lifetime. However, this time they will be held back for just a while longer, for the Earth changes must happen. While souls can be foolhardy at times, they are not so foolhardy as to take a body into the midst of the various disasters to come. Nor would a body be given to them during those times.

This chapter is a chapter of hope. It is a chapter for releasing. Release your fears about death. You have heard many times that death is a beautiful experience. Know that it is. And YES, those souls do come back for their funerals and memorial services. They walk among you and listen to what you have to say about them. So guard your tongue and watch your words, everyone, for the deceased is right there in your midst, listening and enjoying what you are saying (*chuckles*). Sometimes you will get a strange sensation on the top of your head, as if she or he were knocking on the top of your head saying, *yoo-hoo, I am here!*

Do not be afraid. For those of you who have the agreement to make this transition during these next four years or more, do not be afraid. Death is an interesting experience and has many variations to it. You have tried them all and then have settled somewhat on the way you would like—what you have found was the easiest way to be released. This is not so much for the body, but for you the soul so that you can quickly be released.

I cannot think about much more to say about *death*. Actually, *you must experience it in order to know it*. Dear Readers, I hope I have given you a little bit different viewpoint on death. I give it to you simply because you most likely will have relatives, friends, and acquaintances who will be making their transitions. It is inevitable. Just know that they then will be watching all that will be happening on Earth from above, for they will be able to do so.

It is wonderful to be able to speak and teach once again through this Channel, and I am most grateful to her. I greet you. I AM Djwhal Khul.

(*Oh thank you, Djwhal Khul. I was thinking that we needed a chapter on* death *again.*) Yes, people need to have their memories refreshed because every one of your Readers will experience this in one way or another. Thank you.

All right, dear one, that was our friend Djwhal. And it was time to speak on death.

Now, as for the title of this book... As you know it stays the same: The Ultimate Experience, The Many Paths to God. *Now add,* Your Space Brothers and Sisters Greet You, Book SIX. *(OK, I was kind of thinking* **Await** *You...) No, they* **Greet** *You..., for we are coming to greet them, you see.* Your Space Brothers and Sisters Greet You. *(OK, you got it!) Until a few days, dear one, greetings.*

155

Your Space Brothers and Sisters Greet You

CHAPTER 17-ASHTAR-THE SECRET WAVE

Good morning everyone, I AM Yeshua. It is a beautiful morning here in Arizona, and I hope it is where you are also. We are rapidly coming to the close of this book, for this next chapter will be number seventeen. We do roll through these chapters.

This morning we will be having another Presenter. He will speak more on the transporting of humanity aboard the ships. I will let him speak now and come back afterwards.

Good morning, Readers, **I AM Ashtar,** coming back once again to give you more details of this great project we are in the midst of offering you. I first want to reiterate, do not be afraid of us, for we are quite handsome and beautiful to look at! (That is a bit of humor in case you did not catch it.)

We are not some dreadful scary Beings with a dozen arms and legs and different colors, or with huge eyes and little squiggly bodies. NO, we look human just like you, except, if you do not mind my saying so, we are quite handsome and the Ladies (*Lady Masters and Goddesses*) are quite beautiful. It is their beauty inside that is shining forth.

There has been quite a bit written lately about the coming of these spaceships. There have been articles in the newspapers. This Channel last night was watching the Larry King show on television and his whole show was on UFOs. He had different members of a panel discuss the pros and the cons. Of course there always needs to be one who is quite adamant that none of this is true. Those will be the hardest to convince; that's for sure (*chuckles*). However, their disbelief will fall to the wayside when our beautiful ships start landing. Or, when he is beamed up just to surprise him.

Now, how do we plan to do this? This Channel was given much information from me through a reading that she had by Michael Ellegion.. Since it was her reading, we can talk about it and not have anyone think that this was plagiarized in any way. It was information that I personally gave to her through another medium.

I told her that there would be opportunities for humanity to be lifted off when times become rough. Now when I am referring to *times becoming rough*, of course I am speaking about Earth changes. I am not speaking about atrocious wars. Wars are man-made, and we can never save you from wars. Those are your own creations!

We will not allow any nuclear wars, but if you want to have wars and skirmishes and kill each other, remember that that is all part of the dark side of humanity. We cannot save you from yourself. However, if it looks as if a dark one's finger is poised over the red button to trigger a nuclear device, we immediately neutralize it. The button or something else does not work. We do watch very closely, and many times we have interfered with the will of that dark soul. Now, lest you question, we have the permission from the Higher Source. We have the permission of the Creator and the God of this Universe to interfere with man's will when it is turning toward destroying the planet. That will not be allowed.

The Earth is on her way up. She will be advancing just as all of you Lightworkers and Lightweavers will. We make a distinction here—everyone who has love in his/her heart and carries Light in his/her body and carries good thoughts and the love of God for men and women is a Lightworker. They work in your hospitals; they work in your technology departments; they walk among you, or they are your neighbors. They are good people who do not want war. That is how we see a Lightworker—one who carries Light and with a handshake or a hug disperses the Light.

On the other hand, we see a Lightweaver as one who is producing something of Light. Heather Clarke of the Arizona Enlightenment Center created that Center. Therefore, she is weaving Light, you see. She is producing a product—she is a Lightweaver.

She is also the editor of these books and consequently is again weaving Light. Since she is a scribe of these books, we will include this Channel who is also a Lightweaver, for in her many hours of labor and sitting and channeling the different Beings of Higher Consciousness that come to her and then spending hours typing and working on the computer, is she not weaving Light? She is making a product. There are many of you, dear Readers, who are weaving a product.

This Channel has a friend, Jean Alexander, who lives in Arizona and who is also a Lightweaver. She has not written a book, although perhaps one day she may. However, she has a beautiful singing voice. She makes tones with this voice. She is what one would call a *toner* and when she tones, beautiful Light comes forth from her voice and touches the auras of everyone around her. That is weaving Light. Therefore, she is a Lightweaver. Hopefully you can see the distinction that we make here between Lightweaver and Lightworker. Of course they can be synonymous, working the Light codes, weaving the Light into products of Light.

These **Lightweavers and Lightworkers** will be the ones who will be given the opportunity **to be lifted up first.** We are calling it a *Secret Wave* because we are not going to announce when we will do it. These Lightweavers already have the frequency; they carry the frequency in their bodies so that their bodies can be lifted up safely—beamed up safely.

They are all ready. If you are a Lightweaver, do you not think that you carry the frequency to allow you to be lifted up to the ships? *(A rate of 200+ is required. The Masters vibrate at 500+)* Of course you do. It is a necessity that these Lightweavers—I will call them all Lightweavers—come aboard first, for they need to be instructed *(and briefed)*. They need to be educated. They need to be shown the different technologies. They need to visit the Akashic records in the libraries. They need to eat our foods. They need to greet the Masters that are on board the ships. And they need to have time to reflect and rejuvenate themselves.

They will be spending hours in the Rejuvenation Chambers where the DNA/RNA will be upgraded, their cells will be activated. Youth will return. Now when they come out of the Chamber will they look like they did when they were twenty? Most likely not, but they will carry a Light around them that will give them a very youthful appearance. An YES they will drop many years.

You have read, I am sure, that when you are in your etheric body and have crossed over—you have died—you look to be around the age of 35, or when you were your healthiest. This is what is going to happen to these Lightweavers in the Rejuvenation Chamber. That is what *rejuvenation* means—to rejuvenate you.

If you have arthritis in your bones, those bones will be straightened and that dreaded condition will be alleviated. You will no longer have it! If you men have lost the hair on your head, you may find that you have grown hair. Those of you with false teeth will have new teeth (*chuckles*). You will be rejuvenated.

Some of you may be asking, *well what is the purpose for this? Why this rejuvenation while I am still living in a body?* We say, *why not?* You see, your mission is not completed. Your mission is not completed. I will go into that in a few moments, but I wanted to spend more time with you speaking of the Rejuvenation Chamber.

We will have *toning* and Jean Alexander especially will like this one. We will have *crystals* and *color* and *sound*—all of which you are calling *alternative healing modalities*. We have this. Where do you think your ideas came from? All of this we will have in the Rejuvenation Chambers.

Quan Yin told this Channel that when the great doors from the Chamber are opened and your rejuvenated body walks out, you will walk out into the midst of everyone—all the Masters will be greeting you, bowing to you, hugging you, for you have earned it. You have earned it (*said with great emotion*) by the courage that you have had to take this lifetime, by the dedication that you had in signing up for this and by the willingness to do this. And YES, you will be following the Will of God. He too will be there wearing one of His hats. We all will be there.

You will come out the doors in beautiful gowns or appropriate apparel for the men. Your hair will be thicker and shining. You will have jewels on your body. We will give you a medallion or a ring that is tuned to your frequency. When we put this around your neck, it will be similar to the military's *dog-tags*, but it will be fine jewelry. It will be something that you will never take off, for it carries your vibration. It is your entry to the ships at any time. We will give you the formulas; we will give you instructions on how to contact us. And NO, you will not necessarily have chips implanted in your body, unless you wish that to happen.

Picture yourself coming out of the Rejuvenation Chamber looking as you did around the age of 35 or 40. I am talking mainly to the older generation, the seniors, for they have waited so long for this to happen. There will be younger people of course, but it is the older generation, the sages, whom I am addressing right now. Many of these sages are crippled in their hands, in their joints or their knees because of the arthritis. They cannot bend nor walk far, for just living and dealing with the energies of the planet have taken their toll. But they will come back down to Earth as if they have been born again.

The Christians make a big to-do about being born again. They have no understanding of what it is like or the true meaning of it. To be *born again* is to be so full of Light and the Love of God that your body will register that in a youthful appearance. You will be strong and be able to easily walk several miles, hill and dale, without breaking a sweat. You will be so rejuvenated. The older generation will take much pleasure in this. There will be such joy.

How many of you Readers have thought *if I only knew then what I know now?* Well here you will have these seniors with their tremendous wisdom that they have accrued and yet they will have this youthful body. It almost is a reverse position. They will have that youthful body **and** have the wisdom of the sages. It will not only be the wisdom that they carry, but they will carry the Light and Love of God.

After the first group of people—the Lightweavers and the Lightworkers—have been beamed aboard and have been rejuvenated in the Rejuvenation Chamber and have

162

loved and laughed, cried and hugged all the other fellow travelers on board, many of them will meet their Twin Flames and oh, what a grand explosion that will be. After all of that and after they have had their rest and rejuvenation and have received their assignments, they will come back down to Earth to help all of you.

We call it a *Secret Wave* because if we announced it ahead of time, the dark forces in some way would try to sabotage it so that it would not happen. By making it a secret wave of lift-offs, we hope it will be a much wiser way of doing it.

In years past we had planned this, for your Earth was getting very close to being in the midst of her Earth changes, but souls were not ready to leave yet. Consequently, the Elohim were able to stave off the inevitable for many years. But now they have stretched that *rubber band* back so far that it is now time to release it. It is now time to let those changes happen. We are coming up to 2012. It is now time.

After you have the Secret Wave, these Lightweavers and workers will be beamed back down to their waiting and puzzled families. *Where have they gone?* This Channel has warned her daughters that she may be gone a certain length of time, but rest assured that she will be coming back. Her daughters do not quite know what to do with that information, so they have put it into the category of *Mom's World*.

The Lightweavers and workers will have received instructions. They will be given tools to help humanity to be ready. The work that follows, the intensity of it, the danger of it, will be the greatest that they have ever known. We will put great protection around them. As this Channel has said to friends, she is on the *radar screen* where her every move is noted. We note her every move, but as we have said in previous chapters, her privacy is still respected.

Now, I have spoken about the Secret Wave. Lightweavers are beamed up, rejuvenated, greeted, and instructed. They have parties and then they are brought back down. What are they brought back down to do? It is now their responsibility to spread the word to the rest of humanity. They will do that by public speaking. They will do that by publication. Their purpose is to let humanity know that help is on the way.

As I was saying before, if the problem were just wars, we would not be doing this, for fighting it out is man's dark side. The governments are not helping. The word must go out that there is nothing to fear from us. Please, do not try to shoot us down! Do not carry hidden weapons and shoot the first one of us that you see. That would take you back to the dark ages when you would *shoot first and talk later.*

Actually, it usually is the government that gives one the most trouble, for an alarm is sent to the police and the military. The Army and National Guard would roar in with guns blazing and men with megaphones snapping out orders. Half the time, all of this noise from them is what starts the riots and starts getting people trampled. We will not allow that to happen.

We would like you to approach us as you would great cathedrals that are all over the world. When you come to them and step into them, do so with awe and have a quiet way of walking and viewing them. You feel the peace. Approach us as though you were approaching a magnificent building dedicated to God. Our spaceships are Light. God is here. He is with us.

It is our hope that when we land that you will greet us without pointing your guns at us—that we can land and feel your reverence. The Spiritual Beings that will come out of the ships are millions of years old. They carry more wisdom than you as a human can ever imagine. They are highly evolved. And they are good at what they do (*chuckles*). They are very good at what they do.

Each one of your religious sects wants to see Moses, Mohammad, Jesus, Abraham or some of those great prophets of old. Many of those Beings will step out of those ships. They will greet you.

Embrace us, Humanity, embrace us as we will embrace you. Do not be afraid. Our Lightweavers and workers will be well trained and will give you much information. Take it in and do not laugh at it for it is real. They will prepare you. Listen to them. The job description for Lightweavers will be to **educate the public**.

We envision that this may take a year or more and then humanity will be offered the opportunity to be lifted up and off the Earth. That would be another wave, you see, but this time it would be advertised. It would not be a secret. It would be your choice, for by this time Earth changes throughout the world would have started with severity.

If you are in those areas where you cannot tolerate any longer not having electricity or water or food that you enjoy, and you are just tired of all the bad air and the wearing of masks, we are offering you a way out. We will bring you up, or if you will let us land; we will let you walk on board—if you will let us.

Dear Readers, there will be a series of opportunities for you. These are opportunities for you! You will feel like you have gone to *Alice in Wonderland*, for it truly will be a wonderland on board our ships. We have only your best interests at heart. You will feel such love and joy if you but allow it to come in.

That is all I wish to say today, dear Readers. Allow us to help you. Allow us to come into your hearts.

I AM Commander Ashtar, greetings.

(Thank you, Ashtar, that was a wonderful chapter. I was surprised that you talked so much about what you had said to me.) It is time, dear Sister of Light. It is time and you are not the only Channel to whom I will be saying this, for each of you has a different way to get the information out. That is my purpose. This is shared information and it is time. Thank you, Sister of Light. *(You are welcome, Lord, thank you!)* (11-10-07, 10:05 AM)

Well, that was my buddy, Ashtar. He really laid it on the line this time, didn't he? (Yes, if only the Readers will get to Chapter 17, it will blow them away!) It is an incentive to keep on reading, isn't it? (Yes, chuckling.)

All right, let's have our little side-bar here. You are concerned because you are having this rash on your legs. (Yes.) We have told you that this energy that is coming onto the planet is bringing out all sorts of ailments, shall we say on the bodies. (Yes.) This rash is an allergy to what you have been eating. We might suggest that it is too much chocolate, dear one. Can you just stop the chocolate and see if it disappears? Your doctor may say that it is Eczema, or what have you, but that is brought on by incorrect foods. So we say it is from chocolate. Chocolate in moderation is fine, but too much can be poisonous to the body. (OK, will do.)

CHAPTER 18- YESHUA- CHANGE REQUIRED

Good morning once again, everyone—you Readers and this Channel. It is going on 10:00, a beautiful morning on the 13th of November, 2007. I hope we have not lost any of you Readers along the way. Is this information too much for you—too far out in left field, shall we say? Open your minds, Readers; open your minds and open your hearts. Remember, we have said in our previous books that you need to be willing to change. Be willing to change those erroneous belief systems.

I think it is quite difficult for humanity to let go of something that they truly believe in, for if they let go of that belief, something else has to take its place. The something else might be scary for them, so they do not want to replace the old belief system. The new one is too overwhelming. This is about change, dear ones.

Be willing to change and to know that many times it is your ego that is grasping onto the last death throes of an old belief. Remember, one needs to shut the door on one thing so that something else more miraculous can walk through another door. Shut the door on your old beliefs and open the door to change, for it can be so exciting—a new perspective, a new way of walking your truth.

We greet you this morning, dearest ones. I am going to continue this Chapter 18. **I AM Yeshua and The Gang**, for we never come alone. There are many of us here, blending our energies, blending our thoughts, blending our hearts that we turn toward all of you.

You must know by now, truly you must know by now, that you are loved. Truly you must know by now that we of the Spiritual Hierarchy, the Ascended Masters, the

White Brotherhood, all the different names that you have read or heard about, that we have only your best interests at heart. Our hearts are so full of the energy of love. We give this to you. We give you our love. All you have to do is receive it; receive our love, dear ones.

I know that the many comments and suggestions that the various Presenters have given you in this book may be overwhelming to many. For those of you who are just coming into a fuller consciousness, you may not realize what you are up against. You may not realize what you are coming into—a more beautiful planet, a planet that will be able to sustain everyone on it. The planet will no longer have drought, famine, pestilence, and diseases that you are used to having.

Your cancers will not be able to be sustained in the energy that this Earth will have. As you climb up ever more fully, you advance more on the rungs of the ladder of evolution. It is the energy, the frequencies, you see, that do not allow some of these less desirable conditions. They are not able to be in the vibration of the higher dimensions. Therefore, they will just fade away.

However, much of this is predicated on the consciousness of humanity. You need to be willing to change your outlook on life. You need to be willing to receive the higher energies. Much of the energies that are coming onto the planet are full of love, for they are from God. They are from the Creator—energies that we, the Masters, have yet to see. We do not know how this affects the body. We can only watch and observe.

You have had many bodies and ailments in the past. This is past history coming forward. This is your genetic line coming forward, and if you carried these different health conditions from past lives, they are coming forward so that you can transmute them now.

Now it might seem in simple terms I am saying that you can have a rash that is from a past life. *That does not make sense to me*, you might be thinking. But you see, it is the condition of severe skin disorders in a past life that manifests now in the present, today.

If you can alleviate it by not eating whatever is causing the rash, then you are also transmuting the energy so that your body then is becoming more purified. If you have a particular propensity for a particular condition, it will come forth because it comes from the genetic line. All conditions are coming from the genetic line—even if the condition is from pesticides or the water, your body still has the propensity to create those conditions and to be put off balance by them. They stem from the past lives. They stem from way back, even way back in antiquity. They are coming forward.

However, dear souls, embrace the thought that everything has a frequency to it—*everything*. It is all energy. A rash has a frequency to it. The flu has a frequency to it, and the body's genetic line or stream carries the propensities to have this manifest.

Perhaps you can visualize it as a bunch of grapes—a long bunch of grapes; bunches like they have in vineyards. The workers cut off these huge bunches of grapes from the vines. If you can picture that as your genetic line and each grape poses a particular health issue, a particular body issue, then you will have a visual picture in your mind to look at and think about. It will help you with your belief system to see all those different grapes clinging to the main stem—your body—each one representing a different ailment.

There may not only be illnesses, but other conditions like blindness, scoliosis, rheumatoid arthritis, deafness—all of this could stem from your personal *cluster of grapes*. The tremendous force of these energies that are coming onto the planet bombard the bodies causing them to bring forth these different aliments and conditions from the past. They are all ready to be transmuted. Bodies are having a difficult time staying balanced.

It is imperative that you eat correctly and as purely as possible. Seniors are apt to eat too much of the processed foods, for it is convenient and quicker and saves them from long hours of standing in the kitchen preparing meals or from having to run to the grocery store all of the time.

If you are in that category, be sure that when you buy something that is frozen that it is as pure as it can be. Attempt to work a fresh vegetable and a fresh fruit into your menu. Avocados are a wonderful source of vitamins, are easy to prepare, and they fulfill the dietary requirement of having something green. Be sure to eat as healthfully as you possibly can.

We hear your grumblings. We know that you hate to give up your soda pops and diet drinks, your chocolates. We know that (*chuckles*). However, it is harming your body if in fact it is showing some type of reaction. Some people may have congestion in the throat, a sinus problem, or skin rashes. All of these are hints that you are eating something that does not quite agree with your particular body. Each body is different. Someone else can eat that and be fine. However, with your particular body, it may give you a problem.

Now let us leave this little lesson on nutrition that I have given you and move on. I wish to tell you about the food on board ship. Our food is of the highest concentration of vitamins and minerals and all the elements that you would need, not only for a physical body, but for an etheric one. The food is absorbed into your systems. Some of us eat, others do not, but we drink plenty of fluids.

We have a substance that is similar to sugar. It is not harmful to the pancreas in any way if you are in a physical body. We have a wonderful blending of different fruits. We use no dairy products, but we have food that is similar. We can manifest on our ships anything that you have on Earth.

If you want to indulge and have a chocolate milkshake, that can be provided for you! However, it will be of the purest ingredients and non-dairy. It will taste like the best milkshake that you ever have had and create no allergic reactions. Now do I eat things like that? NO, but I do not have a physical body either. I am in my Light body.

We have all of this for you *Earthlings*, shall we say, when you come on board. You see, we realize how much of a psychological effect that food can have on bodies. Bodies, you have heard, eat comfort foods. Some people crave mashed potatoes at certain times in their life. They want comfort food. It seems to bring a soothing effect to the body. Thereby, we have that for you.

We do not feed your addictions. We do not allow the binging, but that would not happen anyway, for the food is so pure that every bit of it is absorbed and you feel satisfied. One milkshake is all that you would want for several days, or any length of time, for the ingredients in our food do not play into the body's cravings. The body just does not crave anything. It is not in its makeup. Everything is made of pure, living ingredients. The banquets we will prepare for you are *out of this world*, if you will forgive me for using that expression. They are out of this world!

Now, dear friends, let us truly leave foods for now. Let us talk about your belief systems. Let us speak some more about that. Do you remember in our previous books that Sananda said that belief systems will form an energy around them that becomes similar to a cocoon? They are impenetrable and you cannot get anything new into them unless the personality desires it.

Many times the soul cannot get the personality to hear it so that it would make the change. Changes must be made in consciousness. For some people, changes only come about when the person is under a great deal of duress, as with grief, mourning deaths in the family, or they have been fired from a job.

Something comes in a dramatic way to them. Sometimes it is joyous, but most times it is not, for the soul is instigating something as a catalyst for change. Many times you will find that it will be people who are the catalyst. I am sure you have heard the advice to not condemn that person for the person could be the *catalyst angel* sent to you just for that purpose so that you would change.

These are hard and difficult concepts for people to embrace. There is no such thing as an accident, as you have heard over and over. It was no accident that you were fired from a job. However, it is a catalyst for change. Those belief systems need to undergo a transformation. They must be transformed, for how else are you going to evolve if you hang on to that which is so old, that which many times is a lie? As we have said in our previous books, are you hanging onto someone else's truth which in actuality is a lie? Are you hanging onto a lie and making it your truth? Why would you do that? Because it brings comfort to you? Because it is in alignment with what you believe?

We also have told you that loyalty will get you into trouble faster than anything. Do not be loyal to someone else's truth, for it could easily be a lie. This is where your discernment must come in—to discern where the truth is. You may start with your heart. Get your head out of the way and start with your heart, for the heart will lead you. The heart must be the master and not the mind. The heart will lead you to truth.

Now what is this truth that I am attempting to give to you so that you will start changing your belief systems? **The truth is, Humanity, these spaceships are coming!** There are people who do not believe in spaceships. They refuse to give a name to them. They call them UFOs, Unidentified Flying Objects. Why do you not just say they are spaceships?

It is quite unfortunate that the movies depict the spaceships' phenomenon as being so scary—the aliens practicing their experiments upon you. Those are not spaceships of Light, dear friends. That is a sub-culture. They are not allowed on the planet any longer. They are not of the Light. They had spaceships that were not of the Light, and consequently they were not constructed in a safe manner. Their ships crashed because their technology, while more advanced than yours on Earth, still was not on an equal to ours—ours of the Heavenly spheres. We are up there; we are up there, dear friends, and we are coming down (*chuckles*), coming down to greet you, as the title of this book proclaims: *Your Space Brothers and Sisters Greet You*; we are coming to greet you. Please, dear ones, please receive us into your hearts and do not be afraid.

I AM Yeshua with The Gang and I bless each and every one of you.

(Thank you, Yeshua.) You are welcome, dear one. We are winding up the book. There will not be too many more chapters, as you know. We have said pretty much what needs to be said. We are coming in a different medium (spaceships) than the public may be willing to accept.

Humanity wants us to come in the glory and shouts of Heaven with the angels blaring forth the trumpets. There will be some of that but not in a religious sense at all. Nevertheless, our ships are truly beautiful (10:30 AM)

(The tape ran out, so we decided to end it.)

CHAPTER 19- LADY NADA- MONEY

Good morning everyone, I am here once again to give you another chapter that we hope will delight you as well as instruct you. So without further words from me, I will step back and let the next Presenter come forth.

Hello everyone, I am back once again. **I AM Lady Nada**, the Divine Complement, Consort of our Lord Sananda. As you know, we are winding up the book. There is not too much left to say, although it has been my experience that people like to have various ideas repeated, for the repetition allows one to separate and to accept, or to ignore, or to make it your truth. Therefore, this chapter is more or less one that you can use to browse through, to see if any of the suggestions we make help you to release some of your old beliefs.

The first concept I would like to bring up is the fact that you are going to come into a time of your life where there will be no more sitting on the fence. You will either make a choice to come with us, or you will not come with us. However, either way there will be a choice that you will need to make.

What you need to look at, dear Readers, is whether your choices bring you delight and joy, bring you to fruition of your soul's purpose, or on the other hand, bring you much duress and all that that entails. We would remind you that for the purpose for this book, we are not dwelling on the dark side. However, there will be much darkness that needs transmuting. This particular darkness for you will have to do with the ill-advised decisions from your American government on the different wars that you have going on on the planet. Not that any of the government officials would read this book, but we would strongly

175

advise not to go charging into Iran as was done with Iraq. Your government has lost its integrity.

Keep in mind that a government is simply a body of people making all the decisions for a particular nation. If you the citizens are having a difficult time with your own issues, having to look at your own egos, your own selfish acts of greed, do you not think that those people in your government are also experiencing similar reactions? That is not a healthy bunch in that Congress. They are not healthy mentally, physically, or spiritually. Now isn't that a thought!

Again, all of the dark in everyone's body is rising up in order to be transmuted. It has to come out, so that you can clear it out and keep it out. These dark thoughts of greed, selfishness, and possession need to be released, swept away by the greater love and Light that you all maintain in your bodies. You just need to bring it forth.

Each of those greedy persons has God's Cell in their bodies—even the atheists and those who are very stubborn in their particular beliefs about different things like the spaceships. They are very stubborn and refuse to change. However, they have that God Cell. If they would but listen to their inner guidance, they might make some wonderful breakthroughs.

As I was saying, regarding Congress and everyone who is making the different decisions to go forth and create another war, this is their dark side coming forth. All they need to do is to say NO to it.

You see, people who have billions of dollars are never satisfied (it was their greed that precipitated Iraq's war). They are afraid that they will run out of money, that they will never have it again! Therefore, they have to keep bringing it in. It is a ridiculous concept. The abundance of

Heaven is just that. It is abundant, but only when you can tap into the correct way of receiving it.

If you receive your abundance through greed, that is abundance coming from physicality. That is climbing on someone else's back so that you can reap the reward. However, those who receive their abundance from God will always have more than enough. It is unending. It will never run out.

This Channel and her daughter, Susan, were putting the book together yesterday. Each had her lap-top, and they were going through the different chapters, finding ways to make this change or that change in the spacing and font. (Towards the end of writing a book, it becomes quite complex. Those of you who have never written a book may not understand this, but it is quite complex and very time-consuming—*the intricacies of framing a book*).

After they had worked a couple of hours, they had a lunch break and sat down at the dining table and just listened to each other. Susan was telling about the fact that her present home with her husband, Charles, had not yet sold. It is a lovely house on the golf course and yet it has not sold. In the meantime they were going ahead with the new house that they were having built and were giving to themselves.

Susan made the comment that people questioned why they would be building a larger home. You see, Readers, this is a case where the souls are going ahead on what they have been guided to do, yet on a personality level they are struggling and they question whether they are pursuing the right course.

As you all know, the housing market has taken a *dive* and people are just not buying homes. Susan was saying to her mother that she had never had problems with

177

money. She had always known that the money would be there. She does not consider herself wealthy, for the money always flowed from long hours of working and on into retirement. She was questioning whether the fact that she has been worrying about their house not selling and moving into a new one in some way had put a clamp on this flow of abundance that she had always had.

After her mother, this Channel, had listened to her, she reassured her that she had been doing all the right things. In other words, spiritually, she still was doing the right things and coming from consciousness and allowing God's Abundance to flow to her.

What she does not realize is that she and her husband are being given a test, a test to see if they can go ahead with their plans and have faith and trust that their present home will sell and that the abundance will come. Consequently, I will put this into this chapter for her, which she does not know yet—that the house will sell and that she has not stopped the abundance .It is continuing to flow to her.

Now, why am I bringing this up in this book? I am using this real-life drama as an example, you see. It is an example of how to stay pure to the knowing when you are in the flow of your Father's Abundance. Or in esoteric terms one could say that *money issues* are not Susan's karma. Each one of the souls has brought in different karma, but if it is not your karma to have a struggle with money, then it will just keep flowing. That has been her case all throughout her life. She also is approaching the age when she will be a senior. She has had many trials where she has had to trust the Abundance of Heaven.

You have members of Congress who have issues with money, while others do not. However, it seems as if those who have issues with money can either have a great deal of money just to see how they can squander it and be greedy and never have enough, or their issue can be that money does not come to them easily and they really have to work for it. To reiterate, when we say that a person has issues with money, it means he or she either will have a whole bunch and will be learning how to handle it, or he or she will have very little and will be learning how to bring more in.

Every soul takes this test on how to handle money as part of its life's learning lesson. When it has learned this, the next lesson may be about trust and believing all is well concerning money. You have heard that expression, *money is the root of all evil*. That is the result when you receive money and do not have love in your heart and you go into greed and power with it. It can turn you darker and can be an avenue where greed or evil can become part of you.

So I have given you this little lesson on *money*. Money is not balanced in this nation. Again, we understand there is karma and some are supposed to have it while others are not. However, there needs to be balance, for it is not meant for people to starve because they cannot buy a loaf of bread.

I have given you some ideas about money to sort and pigeon hole and think about. Having a lot of money can also be a tremendous burden if you do not know how to handle it. People who win a great deal of money through the lotteries many times do not know how to handle it. Your sports stars' contracts give them millions per year, and many do not know how to handle it. It goes toward fancy cars, outrageous pieces of gold and diamond jewelry hanging around their neck, hands covered in huge rings.

LADY NADA- MONEY

Do you think by the year 2011, 2012, or 2015, that money is going to be that important? What would you do with it? You will come into a barter system most likely, for too many people will not have the currency. (I think I would like to name this chapter *Lady Nada's Thoughts on Money*, or just *Money*.)

There is an energy around money. It needs to flow; one must not stop it; one must not hoard it. As soon as you try to hoard it, it stops the flow. You must give it. If you wish to think in terms of *charity*, that is fine. Give to friends or family members, but **give and expect nothing in return except your own joy of giving.**

Some people with a great deal of money will be funding large, altruistic projects. The Light Centers, Light Cities, will cost a great deal of money to build. Those whose purpose is to fund these Centers will be giving millions toward the building of these beautiful places — Cities of Light. They are to expect little in return except their personal satisfaction for having given to God.

One may question how can that be giving to God, when one funds such a huge project — to build a beautiful complex? Any time you give to the betterment of humanity, something of beauty, you are giving back to God. He is in everything. His Energy is in everything and everybody. If you build a beautiful Center and it is built with love, His Energy will be there, for you have given a gift of His Abundance back to Him with love. You have received it with love. There is a flow here of giving and receiving, a flow of energy.

Remember, everything has a frequency. Money has a frequency of its own. You can make that energy one of abundance or one of stinginess, possession, and control. It is up to you, Humanity. You will have many chances in the next few years to think about and relate to the money that comes into your life.

I have gotten off the subject somewhat, but the energy was leading me to say this. The energy of money is all around this Channel; it surrounds her. She will be advised strongly on how to spend it, how to give back to God, and this she will do without any misgivings, we have no doubt of that.

With that, dear Readers, I will step aside, for another one wishes to speak. I will not come further into this book, although I may say a few pages in the Closing Statements.

I AM Lady Nada and I bless you and I entreat you to look at your money situation, mull it over, and make any changes for the positive. Greetings.

All right, dear one, that was our Lady Nada. It was interesting that she spoke of the energy that is surrounding you. And just so you Readers will know what is going on here, this Channel is not a wealthy person. She is not sitting in a palatial house. However, she has a purpose, and it is creating this energy of abundance all around her.

As the energy of money increases, as it comes toward anyone, those who can read auras will see dollar signs. And if it is around a person, it means that money is coming to that person. It will then be up to the person to decide what to do with it.

We will call it a day and the next time we sit it will most likely be for the Closing Statements. Greetings.

(Author's note: As of 11-16-07, the money abundance that Nada refers to is still manifesting for me.)

Your Space Brothers and Sisters Greet You

CHAPTER 20- GOD'S DISPENSATION

Good morning everyone, I am Yeshua. This morning will be the last chapter transmitted for this book— Chapter 20—and then we will commence the Closing Statements at the next sitting. I will step aside for this next Speaker to come forth, for it is His desire to do so. It was His Will to do so. I step aside.

Dearest Readers and dearest Channel of my heart, **I AM** the One you know of as **Father-Mother God.** I wear many hats as I have told you. You could say **I AM Christ Michael** right now. Or, you could just call me **Father.** Or, you could call me **God.** And since the **Mother** is here, **I AM Father-Mother God.**

I speak with you in the last chapter of this book. I wanted to have you leave with the feeling that God is a part of the whole spaceship phenomenon of the lift-offs that will be offered to you. Do you think that these great space Beings would do this on their own? Do you not know that these Ascended Masters are using My Will—that they have turned their will over to Me?

Of course in their own wisdom when they are doing their different projects, it is a combined effort, but they always check in with Me, for it is My Will. They have not turned against Me in any way. Any time that you hear that a Master is doing something, know that it is also God's Will.

For this last chapter, I wanted to make it very clear that it is My Will that these ships come and offer their services. It is My Will to offer this to you, my dearest children. I am offering you a way out of your karma. I am offering you a Dispensation so that you will no longer have to go through those dark contracts. We are tearing up those contracts!

They no longer apply to any of you, once you have made the correct decision to jump down off of that fence that you have been sitting on and come toward Me and the Masters on board the ships. This is my gift to you, Humanity—my gift to you.

Many of you who live in those areas that are right in the path of the Earth Mother's changes—right in the path of Nature's fury—are being given the gift to be lifted up and away. You no longer have to play out that karma. You see, before you take a body, you meet with the various players of your game plan. You meet with your different guides. You sit at a great council table and you discuss your coming lifetime and your past karma and what still needs to be resolved.

You are then given free will choices as to how you wish to live it and how you wish to die. So many of you souls are zealous in your wanting to live those dark lifetimes again and again. You set it up so that you would have theses tremendous exercises, these life struggles. You set it up as to how you were going to be killed.

You see, our dear souls, it is not necessary. I believe it was our Lady Nada who told you it was not necessary to play the same game repeatedly. It is not necessary. I am offering you a gift for a way out. It is My Dispensation for you. I am erasing your karma. You need not go further with it. You need not have repeat performances with it. It is not necessary. You have proved yourselves and now the biggest step that you can take on your evolutionary path is to accept My gift. Do you not see that that is a step in evolution? It entails trust.

GOD'S DISPENSATION

You are saying *I am turning my will over to God.* You are saying *I am trusting Him.* You no longer need to struggle, dear souls. This Dispensation that I am offering you, brings all of your pasts forward. It gives you a clean slate—a tabula rasa—a time in your evolution where you can start over, where you can come into a life without excess baggage.

When so many of you take a lifetime, you come in carrying a huge knapsack on your back. That knapsack is full of your karmic debt: *Who shot whom; who betrayed whom; who gave to whom; who did not receive from whom; who went into greed; who was miserly; who was lazy; who took and never gave.* There are so many games, dear souls, and you brought so much of that with you each time in your knapsack.

Then you say *all right, in the next lifetime I will do better. In the next lifetime I will deal with this karma.* And you bring in all of this karma to deal with again. Sometimes you are able to do it, while other times you cannot. Then you come back to Me and feel that you have failed because you had taken on too much! How many times do you need to be a martyr in a lifetime? How many times do you need to be beheaded for your beliefs? Or hung for your beliefs? Or whipped because you would not denounce Me? You do not need to play that over and over and over and over.

I am giving you the gift of Dispensation. Receive it! Even if you have been unable to receive in other lifetimes, this is the one where you are to receive it (*said with great emotion*). Receive My gift, for it is declaring that you are trusting Me. You are putting your trust in God, the Father.

I have set this whole lift-off drama into motion. I have done this and of course I have worked with the many

185

Masters involved, the Ashtar Command and our Lord Sananda. But **I** am overseeing this! It is **I**, dear souls, and **I** am offering you a little bit of Heaven on board these ships. It will be a respite from the cruel energies that you will feel as the Earth changes become more severe.

The severity is more than you can envision. And yet there will be those stalwart souls who will attempt to stick it out. That certainly is their choice. That certainly is their free will. Do not judge those who decide not to and those who decide to accept my offer. There are always many reasons for such decisions.

Their decisions could be pre-birth agreements. It could be a Master who says *NO, I am to stay here. You go.* There could be Masters who come aboard in that Secret Wave that Ashtar talked about, for many of those Lightweavers are Masters in disguise — many Masters unbeknownst to themselves — for that is all part of their game. That is all to end very soon. People will recognize their self-worth. People will know their lineage, where they have come from.

They will be shocked, perhaps, to find out that they have come from many different planets and even Universes. Do you think everyone on Earth is from the same place? People have come from all over the solar system — from different solar systems, even — they are Star Seeds, a very apropos name.

Dearest Readers, this chapter will be quite short in comparison to the others, but it is loaded with energy and My invitation to join Me and the Masters on board ship. From the moment you enter the ships, you will feel Me to the greatest of your ability.

I believe it was Ashtar who was saying you will feel as if you have stepped into one of Earth's greatest cathedrals. You have no idea what awaits you. And many times that is just what the problem is: people's minds may not be that expansive. They are satisfied in their own little world. A hundred years ago people were satisfied to live on their own little plot of land with just a few neighbors, a little country store, a barber shop and a little cafe. That was all they needed. That was all they wanted. They were not expansive.

Even today there are people who carry that make-up from past lives. They are not expansive. They cannot see beyond the block where they live. They have their TV and the newspapers, but there is no adventurous spirit in them. They are satisfied where they are. Therefore, when something that is tremendously, stupendously, overwhelmingly offered them, such as coming aboard a spaceship, it petrifies them. It just strikes them as if they were in a catatonic state of being. They are so petrified to think of making a choice to come outside of their box. Those souls who are not adventurous could be the very souls that my Dispensation could help the most. However, *they* must take that first step, for it is a step in trust. It is a step in faith; it is a step to receive.

Souls in bodies are not that different from souls in Nirvana. Some are more adventurous than others. Some are quite fearless, like this Channel, for instance. She and her friend, Jean Alexander, joke with each other that at sometime they will need to put *duck tape* on their arms and strap them down, for they are continuously raising their arms and saying *I'll go, Father. Send me, I'll go.* They are the first to volunteer for any magnificent project.

However, other souls are timid, and they carry that into their bodies. This is what makes My world so interesting, as I watch each one of My creations. I would have it no other way. I like the diversity. I like the unusualness. I like the meek as well as the strong, and I love them all.

For now, dear souls, I will say it one more time: I offer you My gift. I offer you Dispensation from your dark karmic debt. I offer you beauty and joy and more magnificence than you have ever dreamed of. Come aboard! I am there just as I am in your world right now. I am on those ships.

I bless you mightily. I hear your prayers and my love for you holds no bounds. Greetings. I AM your Mother-Father God and I AM All That Is. Greetings.

(Father, I am honored, thank you. It is so appropriate that you would have the last word in the last chapter of this book. It is so appropriate and I thank you.) Blessed child, if you only knew the plans I have for you. (*He chuckles a great deal.*) Tape down that arm (*more chuckles*), for you are about to raise it again (*still chuckling*). I love you. I love you. (*Thank you, Lord.*)

Well dear one, I am back. That was pretty powerful, wasn't? (That was a total delight and I had no idea until the last moment when I got the flash, "Oh, my gosh, it is going to be God!" It was wonderful.) Yes.

All right, dear one, the next time you sit, we will be writing the Concluding Statements. Greetings.

CLOSING STATEMENTS- YESHUA - ASHTAR

*Good morning our beloved ones, **I AM Yeshua,** and gathered around me are all of the Presenters that have come into the pages of this book. We are so gratified to be able to do this for you. It is so endearing to us that you will be reading our words. This is the conclusion of this book. These will be closing statements from the various Presenters.*

This Channel had been wondering if there will be another book. We say, but of course there will be Book SEVEN. Do you think we will stop now when we all have our gears rolling so easily? NO, we will have Book SEVEN, but not for a few months. Shall we just say in 2008. And NO, Readers, she does not know what it is going to be about any more than you do! But we know. We already have it up our spiritual sleeves (chuckles).

Therefore, I shall start off giving the first closing statement.

This book has touched on a variety of subjects. However, the main theme was to alert you that your Space Sisters and your Space Brothers are coming. And they are coming to greet you.

Now when I speak about the Space Family, I am including many of the Spiritual Hierarchy. We are on these ships. We have our own ships, That is how one travels around in the Heavenlies, if you wish to use that term. It is very convenient, and we have done it for so many eons of time; that it is our home away from Home. Each of us has different areas in different Universes, even, where we have built our personal oasis. We have let our imaginations run wild in our various creations, which usually entails crystals

–crystal palaces beyond your belief, for we are working with energies.

As we make these Light oases, they beam forth throughout the Universes. They beam forth love and Light. We use different colors. Each of the Masters carries a predominant color. While we are all colors of the rainbow, we have a predominant color. Mine, as Yeshua, is Gold for the Father. Those who are with me in my particular soul group are called the *Golden Race*. We travel together as a huge family of souls in God's Golden Ray.

It is a Ray of Love and Power, but Power used in the correct way. You see, on Earth when people tap into the energy of *power,* they use it in a negative way. Power has its own energy. Just like we were telling you about the energy around money, power too has its own energy. It is a very strong energy. Of course, it is pure power! One must know how to use it. One must use it in conjunction with love, in conjunction with creativity, in conjunction with giving to people. When you make a structure using those concepts, the edifice will be something to behold.

In this book, we have given you a look into the future, for it will be your future when the ships come in, when they land in their sparkling opalescence. They are of beautiful colors—pearl opalescence. Our doors will open and we will step forth.

We have given you much information in this book. There is probably more information given in this book than in all of the other books so far. This Channel is a dedicated soul and walks her truth. We enjoy that saying of yours on Earth—*to walk your talk*—and this she does. We are grateful to her for the many hours she has spent sitting, speaking into her tape recorder, transcribing our words so that they are then on paper, anchored into the world of physicality. This is the purpose.

Every time that truth is anchored in, it becomes a chain reaction that goes around the Earth. You could call it a *domino effect*, for it helps everyone on the same wave length—it helps everyone to make a change.

These books are not only for your edification, but they are to bring you hope for your futures, to give you information that you may not have heard of, to provide instruction of sorts, so that when we land you will know that we come in peace, love, and Light.

We come bearing gifts, for is it not a gift to offer a safe haven in the midst of a storm? Is it not a gift to provide you a safe place to go and to be in our Father's abundance, the abundance of safety, the abundance of love, the abundance of food, the abundance of clothing? Everything that you will need will be provided for you. The Father's abundance is unending. It has no end to it, nor is it stored in a barn so that when the barn looks empty— *that's it folks!* It is unending. It is a continuous flow. Thereby, there can never be any lack on board the ships.

It just will never happen, for you see, so much of what will be given to you is from the energy of loving thoughts. We think it and with our technology, we think it into a machine and it appears for you. If you need a particular bed so that you will feel at home, you express that desire to the helping angel at your side and the angel will think it and it will appear.

Readers, you have no idea, no idea. I am not putting you down in any way. I am simply telling you that you have no idea what is in store for you—the joys that are in store for you.

CLOSING STATEMENTS – YESHUA– ASHTAR

This *still time* today, this *sitting* where we talk to this Channel is on a Tuesday. In two days it will be America's Thanksgiving Day. It is a time when you gather together and give thanks for all of your blessings, joy, and abundance, and your tables are usually groaning with food. Some prepare it all by themselves like going to Grandmother's house in the old days. Or in these modern times the gathering may be potluck where people bring their favorite dish. However, the tables are groaning with food and the leftovers are passed out willingly and with giving love to the various guests as they leave.

It is a joyous time, a time to remember, a time to give thanks; it is a time for forgiveness. Many of you will come to your Thanksgiving tables in the midst of family squabbles. People who do not get along come together more or less out of duty. Never come to a celebration out of duty. It would be better to stay home. Celebrations are just that. They do not need that energy of being forced to go because of a duty versus being willing to go because it was from love.

Thanksgiving is a time for remembering, remembering all that has been given to you for that year; remembering all the good times, the love that has been showered upon you, the gifts that have been given to you and not only gifts of material things, but gifts of the heart—the hugs that your parents or partners have given you; the sweet kisses that your lover has given you. It is a time of remembrance, dear souls. We beseech you to include the Father and the Mother in this also, for they too are part of your Thanksgiving. And always carry forgiveness in your heart. To use Sananda's phrase, *what was, was and what is, is.*

If something was done that upset you and you carry revenge in your heart, release it; let it go. What was, was

192

and what is, is. The *is* is your forgiveness and your love. Do not let it become revenge.

Dearest Readers, it is our fervent hope that you have read every word in this book, for every chapter holds much information, much to contemplate, to ponder and to help you change your belief systems, to help you realize a new truth.

I will now step aside and let the next Presenter come forth, but know that I too am with you and I too will come as I hear you call for me.

I AM Yeshua, Sananda, Esu, Immanuel, Jesus. I bless you.

I AM Ashtar, coming once again to conclude this book. It has been a wonderful experience for us, and I hope it has been for you too. Many of the Readers who email this Channel write that they not only read these books once, but several times, not wanting them to end and asking for further books.

So many of them are waiting for this next book to come out. We hope it will not be too shocking for them and that they will enjoy it as much as the previous ones. You have been reading in the chapters that we will be coming and landing our ships. We will be landing on your shores. But first we will have many fly-overs so that you can get used to us as you look up into the skies and see us.

Once your governments get used to seeing us fly over and realize that we are not there to harm you, we will start landing, making that *first contact* that so many of you have heard about. However, as I have said, there will be that Secret Wave first and then those people, my Emissaries, my ground crew will educate you.

We will show them everything that would be enlightening for all of you. We will show them our technologies, for they will need to be prepared to answer your various questions. *How do you prepare the food? Where do we sleep? What do you do about water? What do you do about body wastes? Where can we roam? Are we restricted on the ships?* All of these kinds of questions and many more we have anticipated, so we will be giving our Emissaries a briefing.

It is not a briefing of just one or two hours, but of many hours and many days. You see, they must have their veils of forgetfulness released. All of that will be done in the Rejuvenation Chambers, for we want them to remember what their life was like on board ship before they took a body. We want their information that has been stored for so long in the cells of their bodies to be brought forth so that they will remember most of what you Readers in the world would like to know.

In this book we have given you much information. We have reiterated much of the information. Can you remember when someone has told you something and you cannot take it all in at once so you say *say that again! What did you say?* You then repeat it to them so that they can grasp it. That is what we did with you Readers.

We repeated so that you could grasp what we are telling you, to grasp the situation, to know it, to read it, to hear it as you read it out loud to yourself in order to grasp what we are telling you. As our Father was telling you, some people just do not have an expansive nature. They are timid souls, so they need to be told several times.

People, after you have read this book, share it with others; loan it out to others; give it away to others, but let people know the information. It can be a grass-roots

194

movement to let people know: *the ships are coming; the Masters are coming.* Let it be a movement, a wave that is sent forth.

We have endeavored to give you what you need to know for now. We have brought you into our inner circle, our inner circle of information so that you too will know not only of the possibilities, but the probabilities, one of which is that *we are coming.* As the title of this book says, *Your Space Brothers and Sisters Greet You*—we are coming.

As I have said before, I speak through any Channel of Light who invites me, for the word must go out. Each Channel has his/her particular network of people that information will flow to. Some have intricate Internet sites and those who read from those sites receive much information, which they then have to discern as to the truth.

Some have radio talk shows and those who listen receive information that way. Others have telephone conference classes and receive information, and then there are those, such as this Channel, who write books and the books are published and sent out across the country. It is our fervent hope that you will accept the information even if you do not agree with it; or even if you *cannot* agree with it. Ponder it. Do not be so swift to slam the covers of this book together.

Many Fundamentalists will find that this information may jar their religious training. Some may go so far as to think this is the *devil* speaking. However, that is their own fear of the unknown. That is their training, for anything that they do not know and seems scary must be from the devil. So much has to be reprogrammed into Beings such as those. So spread these books around, dear

Readers; give them as gifts; share this information, for it is true.

I AM Ashtar of the Galactic Command. Greetings.

All right, dear soul, your body has sat long enough so this will be the last sitting before your Thanksgiving. May it be a blessed one, beloved. Share your Light, peace and forgiveness and love with everyone you meet, as you usually do. Blessings, beloved. (Yeshua, thank you for the wonderful statements from both you and Ashtar. I love this book!) And so do we, greetings, dear one.

(Author: Readers, turn the page as the Closing Statements continue.)

CLOSING STATEMENTS- LORD SUREA - AA MICHAEL

Good morning to all of you Readers and to this precious Channel. It is the day after Thanksgiving and I hope your bodies are feeling satiated with not only good food, but with warm feelings and thoughts, conversation, hugs, and love throughout your day—giving thanks, thanks and giving. That is a beautiful combination.

We continue this morning with the closing statements. I will step aside and let the next Presenter have his say. There will be two Presenters and then I will come back. (Thank you, Yeshua.)

Good morning everyone, **I AM Lord Surea,** back to give you my closing statement on this wonderful book that we all have put together. It is such a joy for us in your Heavenly realms to help write a book. I will put it in those terms, for it not only provides information for you Readers, but it is giving us a great deal of pleasure to make this connection with you, to give you our thoughts on different subjects.

We enjoy this thoroughly, but you see, if this Channel did not offer herself as Conduit, how would we connect with you? We need you. There is that saying *we need you as much as you need us!* Or, we hope that you feel that you need to communicate with the Masters.

This book has preceded swiftly to its final curtain and we are quite gratified. The information that I gave you in my segments were pretty much political in nature. You in America will be coming into, or are in, that time where you will be selecting a new government. I have said quite enough on that subject so I will not reiterate. However, we in the Heavenlies are quite interested to see the desires of the people. We sincerely hope it will be the people who are deciding this contest and not the darker forces who cheat and steal the votes. There will always be some of that going on, even in this next election, but it is hoped that the candidate of your choice gets in.

There is a beautiful future waiting for America in the new world that is being prepared. By that I mean as this dear Earth raises her vibration and traverses through the fourth dimension into the fifth, it will be a new world in consciousness. When so much of the world has been in the lower dimension—the third dimensional thinking where the dark plays havoc on the people's will—it creates such heaviness. Your minds are interfered with and your bodies reflect this conflict. Your bodies are not healthy. Your thoughts are not healthy.

Now I am making a general statement here and I realize that the Lightweavers are in there doing their best, but it is unfortunate that those Lightweavers are not the majority at this time. However, the future of America holds that probability. It will be a future of more Light. The bodies born into that generation will not be so bombarded with negativity. They will not become ill so often. They will not be at the effect of people's negativity, simply because people's thoughts will not have that darkness to dwell upon.

If you are not being bombarded by the media, the media that tells you what is going on in your world, then you are happier for it. If you wake up and it is a sunny day

198

and you have not turned on the news, you will not know that there has been destruction, perhaps, in the block next to where you live. You just see the blue sky and you feel joyous and all is well in your private space.

But then you step out the door and you are into the hustle and bustle of the real world—the world of negativity that needs transmuting. This you are doing and this is why your future will be bright and joyous. The elections will have taken place, Congress will have settled down to getting some business done at long last and all is well with your world. That is our dream for you; that is your future and we hope that that is what your thoughts will bring to you.

You have heard so many times that if you dwell on a certain negative way of being or on a particular dark situation you will draw that to you, for you are creating that whether you realize it or not. It will come into your energy field. However, when there are no more wars and the dark has all but disappeared from the planet, you will awaken and truly feel joyous and blessed.

We can see your future, America, for if we travel far enough out on the continuum, we can see your future. It does look bright indeed, for Heaven has finally made it to Earth! The spaceships are finally accepted. The Masters are finally able to walk your land once again. It will be a wonderful time, Readers. Therefore, do not go into dejection. Keep your spirits high.

We have noticed this Channel, as she acknowledges within herself that she is dwelling on a negative situation in the world, will ask the Father to shine His Light on it and then she says to herself, *I must raise my vibration.* Or she

199

will say to herself, *I must get out of the astral and into a higher dimension,* and she takes some deep breaths and completely changes her attitude and her thoughts. Each time that she does this it does raise her vibratory rate.

She does not put herself into the position where she is not allowing herself to see what is going on around her, but after she has seen it and turns it over to God to bless it or do whatever else He thinks needs to be done about it, she moves forward and refuses to stay in the energy of damning people or the government. It does not mean that she is in agreement with any of the dark actions; it just means she acknowledges what is happening and then she rises above it in her thoughts, which then brings her energy to a higher level.

You see, Readers, you do not need to submerge yourself into the lower energies. See it; discern it and rise above it. Do not keep going back to it, for then you are being pulled back into the third dimensional thinking.

We are adamant about people's need to keep moving forward, to keep walking through this fourth dimension of transition and into the higher levels of the fifth dimension and above. They need to keep moving. You may not realize it, but that is one of the purposes of these books.

Each book brings you to a higher level of consciousness, if you do not get stuck in the fact that you do not agree with this or you do not agree with that and are not willing to stop, ponder, and make a change. Not everyone needs to agree with everyone else, but one needs to discern and to find the truth that lies somewhere in between. There is always some truth in many of the words that are spoken. You have all experienced where someone will make a derogatory remark in a humorous way, showing that person's judgment. Then the person will say *oh, I was only joking.* However, you see there was still truth there.

We have given you much truth in this book. Most of it will be most outrageously off the wall or off the charts for you, but we are aware of that. Get used to us, for we are coming.

With that, dear Readers, it has been my greatest pleasure to speak to you this day. I look forward to meeting many of you in the future, meeting you in the flesh in the future. I bless you mightily.

I AM Lord Surea of Sirius.

Good morning to our Readers, this Channel is trying to figure out *OK, who is next here. We have had Yeshua, Ashtar, Lord Surea; OK who is next here?* I will not keep her or you in suspense any longer. **I AM Archangel Michael**. (*Thanks, Michael, for coming, chuckling.*) Of course, I would not miss this for the world. I just have a few short words to say to you Readers.

It is mainly to tell you to keep an open heart; keep an open mind so that you can make changes in your thought processes; accept us, for we shall be coming. I spoke of the times I would visit the soldiers on the battlefields during the wars. I spoke of the times that I would protect them and keep them from being shot. However, there were times when I too had to step aside, for it was their karmic agreement that they wanted to experience either being wounded or it was the soul's agreement to die on the battlefield.

Death to us is not that horrible, for it is simply walking through another transition into a lighter body. The physical body has dropped its scars from that lifetime. This new world, Readers, that Lord Surea was referring to, will be one of such great joy. It has been a long time before souls could come onto the planet and know it would be a joyous life, versus one of pain and struggle. We are so looking forward to better times ahead.

I have come this morning to give you this short segment for the closure of this book. Keep in your mind that your angels are always with you. If you live in areas that are being burglarized, call upon your angels. They cannot act until you ask them to. However, you can give them carte blanche, as this Channel does.

She gives them carte blanche to protect her and her house; to protect her when she is in her automobile. Give them carte blanche, Readers, to be always at your side and to act on your behalf. We have so many angels that do different services. They are not only angels for protection.

We have angels of mercy for those people who are left behind as their loved ones make their transitions. They show mercy and love and surround the bereaving families.

We have angels that heal and help heal the body when there are illnesses. Therefore, angels have many areas of expertise. Many times if you cannot think of a particular name of a person, etcetera, ask your angels and pretty soon you will get the name in your thoughts. If you cannot find something in your house, ask your angels and pretty soon you will be led to where it is. These angels are just waiting for you to call upon them.

In your new world, you will *see* angels walking on the Earth. You will be able to speak with them, as you would with the Masters. Now it is a ways off into the future, I realize, but you will be able to communicate with the angels. You will recognize them. When you see a person, you may exclaim *oh that's an angel!* And NO, we will not be wearing wings, as I have said, but you will still be able to make that differentiation between a human and an angel standing side by side and walking down the street.

Dear, Readers, open your hearts to the Space Command. They only have your best interests at heart. They only wish to help you, to help you make that physical transition, not the spiritual one (*death*), but that physical one where you actually walk aboard or are beamed aboard the ships. That is a *physical transition*. We are waiting for you. We are waiting to greet you.

Greetings once again, I AM Archangel Michael.

(*Thank you, Michael.*) You are welcome, dear one.

All right, dear one, once again we have had two more Presenters. We will finish this up at your next sitting, which will probably be on Sunday. Until then, greetings.

Your Space Brothers and Sisters Greet You

CLOSING STATEMENTS- TUELLA-DIVINE MOTHER-LADY NADA-YESHUA-SANANDA

Hello once again to our dearest Readers and to this Channel. I AM Yeshua. We are concluding the book this morning. There will be three more Presenters and then I will come back and have the last word (chuckles). So without further words from me, I will let the next Presenter come forth.

Good morning everyone, **I AM Tuella**. (*Good morning, Tuella.*) Good morning, dear soul. We are winding up this book. As you know, we have presented many ideas to you Readers, ideas that you may not have heard about before; or may not even have thought about before; or may not have entered your mind before. Much of what we have told you is in the category of *probabilities*. There are some possibilities in there, but most are probabilities, for the ideas we have given you have been on the Council tables for many years. We could say decades, waiting for this moment when humanity's consciousness is at its highest level that would allow us to land and to make that first contact with you.

Years ago when I walked your Earth and wrote my little books, I was very much in a similar position as this Channel is—channeling every day or so, bringing forth the messages and then going on my missions. It was a joyous time for me. I relished listening to these great Masters. Now I walk among them. Those that I had written about I can now see and I can give them hugs. We communicate with laughter, for we use much humor. We use humor in a kind way and never in a derogatory way, putting someone else down. Our humor is always light and frequently it is silly.

205

CLOSING STATEMENTS- TUELLA-DIVINE MOTHER-
LADY NADA-YESHUA-SANANDA

Readers, I am known for the utterance I use every once in a while, *let's get serious here (chuckles)*. Hence on a serious note, I wish to reiterate that YES, the spaceships are coming. I know it might not seem possible in your present reality. You have heard about UFOs for so long. As Ashtar has said, you have heard about the little grey men and their big eyes experimenting on your bodies. Erase that from your mind. That is not going to happen.

If any work is done on your bodies it is with your permission in the Rejuvenation Chambers. The work can change your cells to their former divine intention. Deformed bodies, arthritic bodies will be straight again. That is the kind of medical work that will be done on you, but only with your permission.

We have so much to show you. It excites me. We so look forward to this happening for you. We are really excited for you. When I walked your Earth, I thought I knew quite well what to expect, but even I was just astounded when I saw the reality of the Father's World.

There is that passage in the Bible *in your Father's House there are many mansions.* I must say, Readers, some of those mansions that are referenced could be the spaceships. Spaceships are mentioned in the Bible, but with a different terminology, for they did not have that vocabulary. They were more often referred to as *flaming chariots* or *shooting stars*. This Channel has found one of the sections in the Bible telling of "flaming chariots." She put it in the Dedication, so read it again, for there is much truth there.

We are just so full of love for all of you. I know you have heard of this before, but oh, you have no conception how wonderful your life will be if you will but trust—trust in the Father; trust the information in this book! Trust, dear Readers, trust. Let it come into your body as truth. When you feel goose bumps, your body is saying *that is truth.*

I do not have much more to say, but I am so delighted and so gratified that I was asked to speak among the pages of this book. Thank you for the privilege of sharing this time with you. Thank you, thank you and I look forward heartily to greeting you as you come aboard the ships.

Greetings, dear Readers, greetings, I AM Lady Tuella. (*Thank you, Tuella, and I am most grateful that you have chosen to come and be a part of this book.*) It was my greatest pleasure, dear one. Greetings.

Good morning once again to our Readers. We are at the conclusion of this book. I come once again to convey my love for all of you. **I AM the Divine Mother,** Mother to all of humanity. It has been such a pleasure to be invited to speak and to have you read my words. You know that you are greatly loved. It does not make any difference whether you are an atheist or not; whether you love my Son or not; whether you acknowledge us or not. It makes no difference.

Dear souls, take heart. The time is very near, very close to when you can come aboard the ships and greet all of us. And YES, I will be there. Of course, I would not miss this for anything that I can think of. This is the greatest happening in the Universe—that the ships are being received on planet Earth. What a joyous moment.

CLOSING STATEMENTS- TUELLA-DIVINE MOTHER- LADY NADA-YESHUA-SANANDA

When the doors of the ships open up, there will be such a burst of Light and love that flows forth. We see many of you falling upon your knees for you will feel for the first time in your life, perhaps, the enormous love that is showered upon you. You will feel as if you are in a cathedral, for you will feel the Father and you will see the various Masters and you will see your Messiahs. It will not make any difference as to what color you are or what type of body you have, for we look at the soul. You are even more colorful on a soul level.

Many of you are finishing up your different journeys through the third dimension, through the fourth and into the fifth. You are bringing your pasts forward. You are transmuting them and it is graduation day for you. It is graduation day, dearest Readers.

You will truly feel the energy that will flow forth as if you were in Heaven, for it truly will be Heaven on Earth. Glorious cosmic Beings in all of their cosmic Light will step forth. For many, the Light will be almost unbearable— exquisitely so—to look at. It truly will be a rapture for the Christians. You will be in awe. You will be wrapped in love, compassion, and joy.

Those of you who read the Christian Bible know that story of Joseph who was sold into slavery by his brothers. Then when famine hit that part of the world, the brothers come to Egypt to buy grain not realizing that the great soul, the governor, second only to Pharaoh, is their brother Joseph. He gathers them into his arms and forgives them and there is such rejoicing, laughter and joy that all is forgiven. That is the way it will be.

All your debts and debtors are forgiven, as the Father was saying by his Dispensation. Walk aboard;

welcome aboard. You are truly now free—truly free from the sins of the body; truly free from the errors of your ways. All is forgiven; come into our arms. The Father's abundance never goes away. Come into our arms and let us greet you.

I am the Divine Mother. My love and blessings I am giving to you this blessed Sunday in November, 2007. Blessings.

(*Oh, Lady, your energy is so beautiful and your message is so lovely. I do not want to let you go.*) My sweet child, I go no place. I am in your heart forever. I bless you.

Good morning, dear Readers, **I AM Lady Nada.** It is a hard act to follow our Divine Mother, is it not? She spreads her love and Light wherever she goes. Our book is finished. There is nothing more that we can say to either convince you or to make it any more real for you. It is up to you now; it is up to you.

In the next few weeks, you will be celebrating that glorious time of year of Christmas Day. Christmas is the time when your Lord anchored the Christ Mass energy upon the planet. He anchored the Christ Consciousness. That is the true meaning of that date.

Christ Mass Eve is a time for reflection—reflecting upon all that is good, reflecting upon peace, upon love and forgiveness and joy and good will to all your relatives, friends, neighbors and humanity. Rejoice, rejoice in the season of giving and receiving. Rejoice, dear Readers.

I have enjoyed my time with you so much and I am appreciative of this Channel, this Sister of the Christ Light.

We have history together (*chuckles*) and it always is endearing to me when I can spend some time with her.

The spaceships are coming, dear friends. Your brothers and sisters of Light will be greeting you. Join us in our celebration, for truly it will be a blessed time in your history when you receive us with love in your hearts. The information in this book may be controversial to some, but take only that which you can joyfully receive and leave the rest to ponder. Do not negate it, for it is true. Do not be a *Doubting Thomas*, for it is true. Make your discernments and change those belief systems. The truth has been spoken throughout this book. I have nothing further to add except to tell you that we are so looking forward to greeting you and hugging you.

Greetings, I AM Lady Nada.

Dearest Readers, **I AM Lord Yeshua-Sananda**. I come to add the last thoughts for this book. Keep that discernment button on, for there is much to discern. There is little that one could say was chaff of a wheat kernel, for all of it are kernels of truth. Just know that the ships are real; that there will be fly-overs. As you see more and more of those happening, watch how your government responds. Watch the attitudes of humanity. Watch the skies, for you will know that the time is drawing near. We will *descend* in order to have you *ascend*. Is not that a beautiful thought—that we bring a bit of Heaven to Earth?

There will be another book but not for a while. The holidays are always time-consuming, but it will give you something to look forward to from this Author. She is a beloved soul and we are deeply grateful for the work that she has put into this book. It is a book from the heart—

from her heart and our hearts to you. As you close the last pages of this book, feel the energy, feel our love for you.

Blessings, I AM the Lord Sananda

All right, dear one, that does it! (Yes, and already I am feeling tearful.) We have come close to you today, so you are feeling the effects of that also. You have much hard work ahead of you, as you know. However, know that we are truly grateful for your dedication to this work. Do you have any questions you would like to ask, dear one?

(No, Lord, but probably when you go, yeah. But for now I am just basking in the energies of everybody. It is so wonderful.) Keep in mind, dear one, I am only a prayer away. (Yes, thank you. I do not want it to end.)

We bless you mightily, our dearest one. All for now, greetings.

(Author: I am feeling very tearful. Grief has already set in! 11-25-07, 10:10 AM.)

Your Space Brothers and Sisters Greet You

EPILOGUE

Readers, Yeshua, the other Presenters and I started writing this book on September 23, 2007. And then, almost two months to the day, November 25, their part in the book was declared *finished*. I can hardly believe it. I have just finished writing my sixth book!

It had been six months since I had completed the previous book, *Messages from the Heavenly Hosts*, and I felt somewhat rusty—as if my *sabbatical* had been too long. However, when I felt that familiar emotion of love flooding my heart, I then knew that this book was starting. I was able to pick up where I had left off.

I disciplined myself to *sit* every other morning, for Yeshua would remark, *I will be back in a couple of days.* It then dawned on me that I was not to channel every day. It worked out well, for it gave me more time to transcribe the tape for that day and then to send it off to Heather, my editor.

The theme for this book was introduced from the get-go. *We Masters fly in spaceships. We intend to come, land, and greet you. We offer you the opportunity to be lifted off the planet—your choice. Have a problem with that? Then don't come on board.* It was as simple as that.

The various Presenters gave us exciting overviews of what life on board the ships would be like—but it always would be our choice to join them there. This was stressed repeatedly. I plan on going. How about you?

Your Space Brothers and Sisters Greet You

ABOUT THE AUTHOR

Verling CHAKO Priest, PhD was born in Juneau, Alaska, hence her name of Cheechako, shortened to just Chako by her mother, a medical doctor, and her father, an Orthodontist. Chako was raised in Napa, CA. She attended the University of California at Berkeley where she met her future husband. Upon their marriage and after his training as a Navy pilot, they settled into the military way of life. They lived twelve years outside of the United States Mainland in various places, which included Hawaii, Viet Nam, Australia, and Greece. Little did she know that these exotic lands and peoples were preparing her for her spiritual awakening years hence?

After her husband's retirement from the Navy, they resettled in Napa, California. It was during this time that she returned to school at Berkeley, transferred to Sonoma University where she earned her first two degrees in Psychology. Chako then entered the doctoral program at the Institute of Transpersonal Psychology (ITP) at Menlo Park, CA, which is now located in Palo Alto, CA. She successfully completed that program which consisted of a Master, as well as the Doctorate in Transpersonal Psychology. Ten years and four degrees later she was able to pursue her passion for Metaphysical and New Age Thought—her introduction into the realm of the Spiritual Hierarchy and the Ascended Lords and Masters.

In 1988, Dr. Priest moved to Minnetonka, Minnesota. She co-authored a program called, *Second Time Around* for those with recurring cancer for Methodist Hospital. She, as a volunteer, also facilitated a grief group for Pathways of Minneapolis, and had a private practice.

She studied with a spiritual group in Minnetonka led by Donna Taylor (*now Fortune*) and the Teacher, a group of highly developed entities channeled by Donna. The group traveled extensively all over the world working with the energy grids of the planet and regaining parts of their energies that were still in sacred areas waiting to be reclaimed by them, the owners. They climbed in and out of the pyramids in Egypt, tromped through the Amazon forest in Venezuela, rode camels at Sinai, and climbed the Mountain. Hiked the paths at Qumran, trod the ancient roadways in Petra, Jordan, and walked where the Master Yeshua walked in Israel.

The time came, November 1999, when Chako was guided to move to Arizona—her next phase of growth. This is where she found her beloved Masters, who in reality had always been with her. They were **all** ready for her next phase, bringing into the physical several books—mind-provoking books, telepathically received by her, from these highly evolved, beautiful, loving Beings. Each book stretches her capabilities, as well as her belief systems. Nevertheless, it is a challenge she gladly embraces.

It is now November 2007. She just has finished writing the sixth book. The Masters are now speaking of the seventh and eighth books. There seems to be no end in sight (*smile*).

Comments and orders:
AZCHAKO@AOL.COM
Chako Priest, PhD
15859 W. Cisa Rio Lane, Surprise, AZ 85374